Decoding Theory of Knowledge

for the IB Diploma
Themes, Skills and Assessment

Wendy Heydorn and Susan Jesudason

Cambridge University Press's mission is to advance learning, knowledge and research worldwide.

Our IB Diploma resources aim to:
- encourage learners to explore concepts, ideas and topics that have local and global significance
- help students develop a positive attitude to learning in preparation for higher education
- assist students in approaching complex questions, applying critical-thinking skills and forming reasoned answers.

CAMBRIDGE
UNIVERSITY PRESS

University Printing House, Cambridge CB2 8BS, United Kingdom

Cambridge University Press is part of the University of Cambridge.

It furthers the University's mission by disseminating knowledge in the pursuit of education, learning and research at the highest international levels of excellence.

www.cambridge.org
Information on this title: www.cambridge.org/9781107628427

© Cambridge University Press 2013

First published 2013
4th printing 2014

Printed in the United Kingdom by Cambrian Printers Ltd.

A catalogue record for this publication is available from the British Library

ISBN 978-1-107-62842-7 Paperback

Contents

Introduction

Theory of Knowledge (TOK) lies at the very heart of the International Baccalaureate Diploma Programme and helps to give the academic rigour that students, teachers, universities and employers value. It encourages learners to put several of the IB learner profile principles into practice: to be reflective, knowledgeable, open-minded, communicative, balanced, thinkers, inquirers and risk-takers.

Decoding Theory of Knowledge is a student-friendly resource that is tailored to the new IB subject guide for TOK. Presented in a clear, concise and highly accessible format, this versatile book can be used in the classroom, for self-study or alongside other TOK texts. It is designed as a practical guide that will enable users to navigate their way through the course by helping to understand both the content and the spirit of the subject and to decode the assessment requirements of the course, thus helping to raise achievement in TOK assessment tasks.

The book provides tools to explore different areas of knowledge and investigate the different ways of knowing that they rely on. The tasks throughout the text are aimed at developing critical thinking and analytical skills. These skills will not only help students in performing well in TOK assessment but will also deepen understanding of other DP subjects and be invaluable throughout life. The book addresses central questions including:

- What is knowledge?
- What is a knowledge question?
- What is the difference between shared and personal knowledge?
- How can I compare different areas of knowledge?
- What skills do I need?
- How will I be assessed?

Unit One challenges ideas about knowledge and investigates some of the ways in which knowledge can be classified. It raises questions about the nature of knowledge and the certainty of knowledge claims.

Through its discussion of the IB's eight ways of knowing and eight areas of knowledge, **Unit Two** helps to discover new connections between areas of knowledge, and enables students to develop a richer understanding of these connections. It is recommended that students study six areas of knowledge and four ways of knowing.

Units Three and **Four** offer practical advice on the TOK assessment tasks and how to complete them successfully. The assessment criteria for the essay and presentation are fully explained.

Features of the book

The key features of the book are as follows:

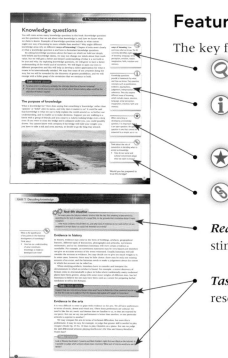

- 🔍 to define *key terms* to enhance students' understanding of the text.

- ⓘ to provide further information on *key points* to support students' understanding.

- ★ to provide hints and tips to decode concepts, skills and assessment.

- 🔗 to highlight knowledge framework links to other areas of knowledge.

- *Real-life situation* boxes to present a real-life scenario offering students a stimulus for further thinking and exploration.

- *Task: think about* and *Task: activity* boxes to engage students in analysis, research and discussion, providing tools for critical thinking.

The end-of-chapter sections for Units 1 and 2 include the following:

- *Knowledge questions* to provide thought-provoking questions to broaden horizons and develop thinking skills.

- *Presentation tasks* to offer clear guidance on how students can plan and deliver a successful presentation.

- *Extended writing tasks* to help in enriching the quality of students' written work.

- *Prescribed essay topics* to provide sample assessment questions from past papers.

- *Further reading* to provide details of extra resources that will help students gain a wider perspective of the topic.

The end-of-chapter sections for Units 3 and 4 include the following:

- *Summaries* to provide a quick reference to the main points addressed in the chapter and *checklists* to help with essay and presentation planning.

1 Types of knowledge and knowledge questions

Introduction

The concept of knowledge is difficult. On the one hand we commonly speak of knowledge and what we know, and we take it for granted that everyone who understands our language understands what we mean when we say we know something. On the other hand, when we try to say exactly what knowledge is, we find ourselves struggling. Yet it is an exciting struggle that will take us on an intellectual journey, during which we will develop our skills as reflective thinkers and gain a much richer understanding of the world.

We frequently make **knowledge claims** about the past. We might, for example, say we know that Neil Armstrong was the first man to walk on the moon. In saying this we are claiming knowledge that is based on what our parents and teachers may have told us, or perhaps what we have read in books or on the internet or (if we are old enough) what we saw on the television in 1969. It is a knowledge claim that is widely accepted among the majority of societies around the world.

Yet we cannot say that all societies accept it as knowledge because there may be some ethnic groups who have never heard of the 1969 moon landing. Neither can we say that everyone who is aware of the knowledge claim accepts it as true, because there are a number of conspiracy theorists who claim that the Apollo mission was an elaborate hoax. Unless we were party to the Apollo 11 mission, we may not be able to say with *certainty* that Neil Armstrong was the first person to walk on the moon, but we can say that it is a claim accepted by the majority of the world to be true, and it is generally regarded as a part of the vast collection of knowledge we have about our past. If we were to enter a quiz and were asked 'Who was the first person to walk on the moon?' the expected answer would be Neil Armstrong, and if we can give that answer, we say that we *know* it.

We also make knowledge claims about the present. We may say that we know Paris is the capital of France, or that the country that was once known as Burma is now known as Myanmar. When considering knowledge claims, we recognise a difference between somebody saying 'I *know* Burma is now called Myanmar' and saying 'I *believe* Burma is now called Myanmar'. The first is a claim of personal certainty: it is true that the country once known as Burma is now called Myanmar, and I am certain of this. The second claim recognises a personal uncertainty: I think it is true that the country once known as Burma is now called Myanmar, but it is possible I may be mistaken. Therefore, we can say the claim to *know* is linked with

knowledge claim: a statement in which we claim to *know* something. For example, 'The universe is 13.77 billion years old' is a knowledge claim made by many physicists. It may or may not be true.

A knowledge claim can also be a claim made about knowledge. For example, 'knowledge can be based on faith and reason'.

A knowledge claim can also be a claim made about knowledge. For example, we know Neil Armstrong walked on the moon because we have faith in the truthfulness of the NASA scientists, astronauts and media who reported the event. This is a claim that knowledge can be based on faith.

subjective certainty. In other words, when I say I know something, I am claiming to be certain about it. But if we cannot be certain what we mean by knowledge, how can we claim to *know* anything?

Task: activity

1 Identify one or two examples of knowledge claims made in each of your IB subjects.
2 Do they have anything in common?
3 Can your examples help you to identify more precisely what we mean by knowledge?
4 Is there a link between the certainty of a knowledge claim and the area of knowledge it comes from?

Task: think about

There are many answers to the question 'What is knowledge?' One answer put forward by the ancient Greek philosopher Plato is that knowledge is 'justified true belief' (although Socrates refutes it in Plato's *Theaetatus*). What are the strengths and weaknesses of this definition?

The example of the Apollo 11 moon landing illustrates the difficulty of certainty. Although there may be an enormous body of evidence to support the truth of the claim that Neil Armstrong walked on the moon, there is a considerable minority of people who, for various reasons, believe that this evidence is insufficient and unreliable. Unless we have privileged access to the evidence, or were personally involved in the Apollo mission, our claim to know that it happened ultimately comes down to 'whom do we trust?'

Plato's definition of truth, '**justified true belief**', is rather circular. We may call certain propositions knowledge because we have good reasons to believe them to be true (in other words they are justified beliefs) but this does not overcome the difficulty of how we know them to be true.

For example, I may believe I hear my dog barking in the garden. I may be justified in believing this because I have a dog who has a deep bark just like the bark that I can hear. But I can only say that it is true that my dog is the dog that was barking if I know for a fact that it is indeed my dog barking, and not the dog next door or any other dog that may be passing by my house. Hence I must know it to be *true* before I can claim to *know* it.

If I claim to *know* my dog is barking, my claim is based on a justified belief, which may or may not be true. Nobody would want to define knowledge as 'justified *false* belief' so it is hard to see what essential role the word *true* plays in the definition in this case.

There are times when we may want to make a knowledge claim about some future event. For example, I might claim to know that the 2016 Olympic Games will be held in Rio de Janeiro. My belief is justified by the media reports that have declared Rio de Janeiro was selected to host these games by the International Olympic Committee. If, in 2016, Rio de Janeiro does indeed host the games, my knowledge claim will be validated as true. Does that mean I can claim to *know* the venue for the 2016 games now?

justified: shown to be fair, right or reasonable

true: logically consistent, honest, correct or accurate

belief: a feeling that what you think is true

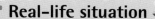

Real-life situation

A highly trained meteorologist, having studied the weather patterns carefully, made a claim based on strong evidence that it would rain the next day. It would seem reasonable to call the forecaster's belief that it would rain a justified belief.

The next day, despite the presence of heavy rain clouds in the sky, no rain actually fell, so it was said that the forecaster had a justified false belief, and people reached the conclusion that the meteorologist therefore did not *know* it was going to rain when he made his forecast.

- If it had rained the following day as the meteorologist had said, his justified belief would have been a true justified belief. But could we really say in this case that the forecaster *knew* that it would rain?
- Is a prediction based on strong evidence the same as knowledge?
- Even if he did know, how useful is such knowledge if we only know after the event that the meteorologist *knew* rather than merely *believed* it would rain?

Think about the role of language when making knowledge claims about knowledge.
- What do we understand by key concepts such as opinion, belief, fact, certainty and knowledge?
- What role does convention play in our use of these terms?

We may be able to decide on the truth or falsity of a predictive knowledge claim because either it happens or it doesn't. But, as we have seen in the case of the weather forecaster, this knowledge is not very helpful. If we ask someone whether the next train will take us to Mumbai, we want to be sure that person knows the answer *before* we board the train. There are some really difficult philosophical arguments about whether we can know the future in any useful sense of the word *know*.

Task: think about

- What if the prediction is almost certain? For example, can I say that I *know* that if I hit this crystal vase forcefully with a sledgehammer, it will break? Or that if a rocket made of any materials currently known to us were sent to the Sun, it would burn up before reaching it?
- What about the statement that I *know* that I will die one day?

Although a very popular and famous claim, 'justified true belief' has serious deficiencies as a way of defining knowledge; we need another way to evaluate knowledge claims.

Types of knowledge

It is helpful to divide knowledge into different types: there is no best way to do this. We might divide knowledge into *a priori* (before experience) and *a posteriori* (after experience); or we might prefer to divide it into first-hand knowledge (knowledge we gain for ourselves) and second-hand knowledge (knowledge we acquire from other sources). In Chapter 3 we will consider knowledge as shared and personal, but in this chapter we will divide knowledge into three types: practical knowledge, knowledge by acquaintance and factual knowledge.

Practical knowledge

Sometimes we know how to do things but are unable to say how we do it. For example, we might say a gymnast knows how to do a triple somersault if he can perform it, even though he may find it difficult to explain how he does it. **Practical knowledge** is necessarily personal; although many of us may know how to play a violin, each of us will bring something unique and personal to that skill. We will discuss personal knowledge further in Chapter 3.

practical knowledge:
the kind of knowledge we have about how to do things, like how to swim, play a violin or read Mandarin

Task: think about

- With every skill we have, we could spend a lifetime improving upon it and learning more about it. At what point can we say we know how to perform a practical skill? For example, how large a vocabulary do we need to have before we can say we know how to speak Swahili?
- Can we say we know how to swim if we can only swim one metre? What about if we can swim half a length of a swimming pool?
- How proficient do we have to be on the violin before we can say we know how to play it?

Knowledge by acquaintance

Knowledge by acquaintance is the personal knowledge we have first hand. It can include knowing ourselves, people we have met, places we have been to, or the taste of things we have eaten. It can also include knowledge that we acquire through reasoning. Of course our knowledge by acquaintance can be flawed. We can be mistaken about ourselves, as well as about people we have met.

As with practical knowledge, we do not have to be able to explain knowledge by acquaintance. In other words, I can say I know what chocolate tastes like even if I am unable to describe the flavour, or I know Lake Taupo, even if I cannot give you any information about it.

Task: think about

- What do we mean when we say we know a person?
- To what extent can others know us better than we know ourselves?
- How can we be acquainted with people for a long time yet never really *know* them?
- If I say I know what chocolate tastes like because I have eaten lots of it, it may be true that I have eaten lots of it, but who can say whether or not it is true that I *know* what it tastes like?

factual knowledge:
knowledge about events that have actually occurred or things that have been verified as true

areas of knowledge: branches of knowledge that have a distinct nature and different methods of gaining knowledge. The IB currently recognises eight areas of knowledge: mathematics, natural sciences, human sciences, history, the arts, ethics, religious knowledge systems and indigenous knowledge systems.

Factual knowledge

Factual knowledge is the collection of knowledge claims about the world that we believe to be true, and these are arguably the most problematic of all knowledge claims in all **areas of knowledge**.

At a trivial level, some factual knowledge claims are true by definition. An example of this is 'My parents are my mother and father.' The definition of the word 'parent' is a mother or father, so the claim can be regarded as a *fact* of the English language. However, there is no guarantee that a truth by definition entails existence. For example, we can *know* that 'a unicorn is a horse-like creature with a single horn rising from its forehead', but this does not necessarily mean that unicorns exist.

However, relatively few of our knowledge claims are based on definitions. Far more are made on the basis of our sense perceptions, emotions, faith, reason and memories. These all contribute to first-hand knowledge. Of course, only I know what I can see, hear, taste, smell, touch, feel or remember, and there is always a possibility that I might be mistaken.

The problem is compounded further when we consider that most knowledge claims are made on the basis of somebody else's sense perceptions, emotions, reason and memories. Think about what we learn at school. Some of it will be through our own discoveries, perhaps in the science laboratories, but most will come from other people: our teachers, friends, news broadcasters, authors of textbooks, newspaper articles or websites, and so on. This is all second-hand knowledge. How can I *know* that their claims are true, even if I accept that they have well-justified beliefs supporting their claims?

In what sense do you think unicorns exist?

Task: think about

- Do unicorns 'exist'?
- How we answer depends on our understanding of language and the way that we use the word 'exist'. We can extend this to other concepts. For example, do ideas exist? What about minds? Or souls? In what sense do colours 'exist'? Can we really *know* about things that don't exist?

Task: activity

1   Consider the following knowledge claims:
   a   I know how to ride a bike.
   b   I know the time is 2 p.m.
   c   I know my mother loves me.
   d   I know how to read Hebrew.
   e   I know my way home.
   f   I know Barefoot Cafe serves good food.
   g   I know Leonardo da Vinci painted the *Mona Lisa*.
   h   I know William Shakespeare wrote *Hamlet*.
   i   I know eggs are a healthy food.
   j   I know gold is a naturally occurring, soft, shiny, yellow metal.
   k   I know my brother has a scar on his right arm.
   l   I know that the Earth revolves around the Sun.
   m   I know a square is a quadrilateral with four equal sides.
   n   I know Madrid is the capital of Spain.
   o   I know I have a toothache.
   p   I know that Lee Harvey Oswald shot John F. Kennedy.
   q   I know that water is made up of two atoms of hydrogen and one atom of oxygen.
   Which are examples of practical knowledge? Which are examples of knowledge by acquaintance? Which are examples of factual knowledge? Which are true by definition?
2   How many are first hand and how many are second hand?
3   Which can we say with certainty are true? How many could be mistaken?
4   Are there any claims here that you would say we cannot know? Are there some that you would say we know, even if we cannot be certain they are true?

Compare the roles of reason, emotion, sensory perception, imagination, memory, intuition and faith in generating knowledge about knowledge.

- Are some of these ways of knowing more important than others in generating knowledge about knowledge?
- How do we distinguish what we know from what we believe?

Think about the role of convention in deciding what to accept as knowledge.
- How do our social and cultural conventions shape what we claim to know?

We need to think about knowledge differently. We may want to say knowledge is the set of beliefs we rely on when living our lives. In this case, we may treat some of our beliefs as knowledge if we think they are reliable enough to be used to help us evaluate other beliefs. Knowledge, then, is the set of beliefs that we trust. We may not be absolutely *certain* they are true but we treat them as if they are because they are the best we can do right now.

Task: think about

- Related to this view of knowledge is the position that knowledge is what a society agrees upon as knowledge. Is this the same as saying that truth is what societies agree upon?
- What is the difference, if any, between saying 'I am certain' and 'It is certain'?

Of course, different societies have different sets of beliefs that they trust and live by, and therefore different ideas about what should be regarded as knowledge. One group of people may agree that their ancestors watch over them and influence, or even control, what happens in their daily lives. If this is regarded as true by that society, it will shape the ways in which the members of that society live their lives and the 'knowledge' they pass on to their children. Another society may think that there is no such thing as a spirit world and dismiss any talk of supernatural things as superstitious nonsense. Again, this will shape the ways in which members of that society live their lives and the 'knowledge' they pass on to their children.

This brings us to the difficulties of relativism. People who hold a relativist position want to say that what is true for you is your knowledge, and what is true for me is mine; both are of equal value and both have equal status as knowledge. It is a claim we often hear, but few who say it *really* believe it.

valid: well-grounded or justified

Task: think about

- If 'Pigeonalians' claim to 'know' that males are superior to females in every way, and use this 'knowledge' to treat the women among them as livestock, would we really believe their 'knowledge' is as **valid** as the knowledge of societies which regard men and women as being of equal value?
- Or if 'Daisinicians' claim to 'know' that the only way to keep their gods happy is to sacrifice all first-born children, would we be prepared to say that this 'knowledge' is true because it is true for them?
- Or perhaps a political group 'knows' it has the only 'correct' political policies on the planet. And they 'know' that they have a duty to fight until every country has adopted their political system. Are we really going to say that their 'knowledge' is to be respected as much as anyone else's?

Although the three examples may seem rather extreme, they make the point that the relativist's position is not good enough and in practice nobody really adopts it consistently. To claim that all knowledge claims have equal value is a ploy to avoid the very difficult and sometimes sensitive task of evaluating knowledge claims individually.

This is one reason why **knowledge questions** need to be asked.

knowledge question: an open question that explores issues of knowing

Knowledge questions

You will come across many knowledge questions in this book. Knowledge questions are the questions that we ask about what knowledge is, and how we know what we claim to know. Examples of knowledge questions include: to what extent might one way of knowing be more reliable than another? Why might different knowledge areas rely on different **ways of knowing**? Unit 4, Chapter 18 looks more closely at what a knowledge question is and how to formulate knowledge questions.

By asking knowledge questions about the bases on which we hold our deeply held beliefs and knowledge claims, we may not change our minds about their truth value, but we will gain a better and deeper understanding of what it is we hold to be true and why. By exploring knowledge questions, we will grow to have a better understanding of the world and of ourselves. We will begin to open our eyes to different perspectives and this will help us develop a richer appreciation for what it means to be internationally minded. We may lose some of our *certainties* along the way, but we will be rewarded by the discovery of greater possibilities, and we will emerge with a fuller grasp of the certainties that we continue to hold.

> **Task: think about**
>
> - To what extent is achieving certainty the ultimate objective of human knowing?
> - If we were to decide that we can only be certain about trivial matters, what would be the objective of human inquiry?

The purpose of knowledge

What is knowledge for? How does saying that something is 'knowledge' rather than 'opinion' or 'belief' alter its status, and why does it matter to us? It could be said that knowledge is what we use to help explain the world around us, to further our understanding, and to enable us to make decisions. Suppose you are walking in a forest with a group of friends and you come to a rickety-looking bridge over a deep river. If you were to cross the bridge and it collapsed under you, you could possibly drown. You cannot know with certainty if the bridge will hold your weight; you just have to take a risk and cross anyway, or decide to go the long way around.

> **ways of knowing**: how we know what we know. The IB currently identifies eight ways of knowing: language, sense perception, emotion, reason, imagination, faith, intuition and memory.

> Knowledge questions provide a framework for what and how we know. They examine concepts such as justification, evidence, assumptions, judgement, interpretation and coherence. They also explore different ways of knowing, which include reason, emotion, language, sense perception, imagination, intuition, faith and memory.

> When extracting or developing a knowledge question, it is important that it is an open question. An open question is one that cannot be answered by a simple *yes* or *no*.

Would you be prepared to trust this bridge?

Try to be precise in your use of language. Do not call something a 'fact' or 'knowledge' if it is really an 'opinion' or 'belief'.

Task: think about

One member of your party says, 'I know this bridge will take my weight.'
Another member of the party says, 'I know this bridge. It was built by my grandfather.'
- Both knowledge claims may be made by trusted friends, but how useful are they?
- If you are thinking about crossing the bridge, the reliability of the first knowledge claim may be crucial but how can you know if it's true?
- Can you think of a situation in which the reliability of the second of these claims might be more important than the reliability of the first?
- How important is it that knowledge with life-shaping importance has social approval and acceptance?

What generally matters is the *extent* to which something is accepted as known or true by society rather than *what knowledge is,* or *what truth is.* It is unlikely that we will ever be able to agree upon anything non-trivial that is true for all people in all places at all times. A seemingly 'true' statement such as 'The Sun rises and sets each day' is only true from an earthly perspective. Astronomy teaches us that the Sun does not really rise and set, instead, the Earth travels around the Sun. Whether or not the Sun appears to rise each day, and the extent of any rise, depends on where observers are located and the time of the year. What we can say is: *our knowledge is the best we can do right now* given that we are a particular group among a particular species in a particular place and time.

The reason for this practical approach is that we cannot suspend our judgement endlessly while we await an absolute certainty that comes through possessing perfect information: we have to get on with our lives; we have to act; we have to decide. If what we are deliberating about has no consequences for our action, it has little importance whether we construe it to be 'knowledge' or not.

Task: think about

Read the following knowledge claims:
a Sheep remember faces.
b Genetic material is made up of DNA molecules.
c Abraham Lincoln was assassinated on 14 April 1865.
d Kashmir is a disputed territory.
e The polar ice caps are melting.
They are claims that you may or may not accept as knowledge. How you regard the importance of the truth of each of these claims will probably depend on who you are, what you do, where your interests lie and which society you belong to.
- Do you agree? What follows?
- Think of some knowledge claims that are important to you. Do you think they would still be important to you if you had been born into a different family or in another country?

You may be coming to the conclusion that knowledge is a very difficult concept to pin down. Theory of Knowledge (TOK) helps us appreciate what matters so that we learn to deal with knowledge claims in a way that shows some awareness of the difficulties and dangers of treating things as knowledge without question and without good reason.

In every subject in the IB Diploma Programme curriculum we encounter knowledge claims, and these claims usually come with powerful support from a complex mix of tradition, authority, practice and educational reinforcement. But we should at least remember that claims to knowledge always come with these attributes, and before the modern era, similar claims were made in the name of what we now regard as discredited scientific worldviews, religious prejudices, superstitions, errors and lies.

The knowledge matrix

So far we have looked at knowledge claims largely in terms of individual statements, but very few important knowledge claims arise in isolation; most are part of a complex web of ideas and claims about the world that we constantly cross-reference using a skilful set of tests and resources to see whether they are consistent with each other. Knowledge therefore consists of a *matrix of concepts, facts and relations* that we rely upon as a whole when assessing any individual claim we come across. Whether faced with a knowledge claim we need to ask questions such as:

- For whom is this true?
- On what grounds is it claimed to be true?
- Does this knowledge claim cohere with or contradict knowledge claims that I already believe to be true?
- To what extent does society rely on this claim being true?
- To what extent can I rely on this claim being true?
- What are the consequences of accepting this claim as true?
- What difference does it make whether I regard it as certain or not?
- What are the consequences I might face if I do not accept the truth of this claim?

knowledge matrix: a network of intersecting ideas, beliefs and facts within which new knowledge arises and develops

Real-life situation

Three friends in Florida, USA, claimed to have seen an alien near a bridge around 11 p.m. on 21 March 2012. They claim the streetlights began to flicker strangely just before the alien came into view. The alien is said to have been over 2 metres tall with fluorescent eyes, and was seen dragging a large bag. One of the witnesses later sketched the alien.

- We would probably accept the eyewitness accounts of three people who claimed to have witnessed a crime, but many people may be reluctant to accept an eyewitness account of an encounter with an alien. Why?
- Eyewitness accounts are based on sense perceptions and memory. How reliable are these ways of knowing?
- Would it make a difference to your willingness to believe the story if one of the witnesses was your best friend or a family member?
- What would it take to convince you that the alleged sighting was real?

When investigating any issue, always consider claims and counter-claims.

Knowledge questions

- To what extent must an individual's certainty align with public knowledge (knowledge that is widely shared across a community) before his or her knowledge claims can be accepted?
- To what extent does our willingness to rely on eyewitness accounts depend on our emotional responses?

Presentation task

Consider how you might develop the second knowledge question above for a presentation. What other real-life situations might your developed question apply to?

Extended writing task

Write 500 words on one or both of the following questions:

1 How important is it that we are certain about what we claim as knowledge?

2 To what extent might it be more important for knowledge to be useful rather than accurate?

Prescribed essay titles

1 How can we recognise when we have made progress in the search for knowledge? Consider two contrasting areas of knowledge. (November 2010 and May 2011)

2 'There are no absolute distinctions between what is true and what is false.' Discuss this claim. (November 2010 and May 2011)

3 Compare and contrast our approach to knowledge about the past with our approach to knowledge about the future. (November 2008 and May 2009)

Further reading and sources

Ayer, A.J. 1961. *The Problem of Knowledge*. Penguin.

Pritchard, Duncan. 2006. *What is This Thing Called Knowledge*? Routledge.

Samuels, Raymond. '*Extraterrestrials: Florida witnesses report alien, unusual eyes*' Digital Journal, 29 April 2012.
    Available at: http://digitaljournal.com/article/323874

2 Justification and evidence

Introduction

We came across the word 'justified' in Chapter 1 when we considered 'justified true belief' as a definition of knowledge. Although we saw many difficulties with this definition, the principle of justification is important when we are trying to evaluate a knowledge claim. We may, for example, want to ask ourselves 'Is this knowledge claim justified?' By this we mean 'Is this knowledge claim supported by substantial evidence and/or valid reasoning?'

Reason can be a confusing term because it is used in a variety of closely related ways. There is *reason* as an IB way of knowing, which describes a number of logical methods of structuring arguments, such as inductive and deductive *reasoning*. A logical, well-structured argument might be called a *reasoned* or a *reasonable* argument.

We can also use the word *reason* to mean a cause. For example, I might say 'the *reason* I am late is my car broke down.' Sometimes we use the word *reasonable* in this sense. If we say something is *reasonable* we are saying that we have cause to accept, believe or agree with it. For example, we might say, 'His illness was a *reasonable* excuse for his absence.'

Evidence is an important factor when trying to decide whether anything is justified. We may need to ask ourselves, 'Do we have enough evidence to justify this claim?'

One of the suggestions to emerge from Chapter 1 was that knowledge consists of claims that are 'the best we can do right now' rather than absolutely certain and incontrovertible truths. How comfortable are you with this definition of knowledge? Think carefully about it, because changing what we regard as knowledge may have a significant impact on what we are prepared to regard as a justification for that knowledge.

> ⭐ When using words that have different meanings, you need to clarify your terms and be consistent in your use of them.

Task: think about

- When we justify a knowledge claim, to whom are we justifying it?
- Do we need the same quality or quantity of evidence to justify it for others as we need to justify it for ourselves?
- If knowledge is 'the best we can do right now', how might this affect open-mindedness? What about international-mindedness?
- To what extent might this view of knowledge justify relativism?

What is justification?

In Chapter 1 we were introduced to a simple definition for the word 'justified': 'shown to be fair, right or reasonable'. But each of the words in our definition is also problematic. What do we mean by 'fair'? I am sure we can all think of times when we have disagreed with a parent or a teacher. For example, my parents might have said that I could only go to the cinema with my friends if we took my little brother with us. What they may have thought was fair I might have regarded as 'unfair'. We all have different ideas about what being fair is. Often these views depend on the circumstances and to whom one needs to be fair. We may be far more generous in our understanding of fair treatment when it involves people we like; we may be far less generous in our interpretation of 'fair' when it involves people we mistrust.

Task: think about

- What do you understand by the word 'fair'?
- Where does 'fairness' come from? For example, is nature 'fair'? Is life 'fair'?
- Do we rely more on reasons or emotions when deciding what is fair?

The word 'reasonable' was also used in our simple definition. For something to be reasonable it needs to be based on reason. Of course, many things can be based on reason and yet still be wrong: for example, if I know that hot air rises, I might reason that the higher I am, the hotter it will be. This is wrong because it fails to take into account many other factors that affect temperature such as the condition of the atmosphere.

Real-life situation

If it normally takes me 20 minutes to drive to school and one day I leave home 10 minutes later than usual, it might be *reasonable* to assume that I will arrive at school 10 minutes later than usual. But it may be that leaving 10 minutes later makes me 30 minutes late because of extra traffic on the road.

- Could I be justified in assuming I will be 10 minutes late if I leave home 10 minutes late?
- If I know there is likely to be more traffic on the road when I leave home late, could I be justified in thinking I will only be 10 minutes late?
- If I am punished for being 30 minutes late when I only left home 10 minutes late, is that punishment justified? After all, the other 20 minutes weren't my fault, were they?

A justified opinion is one that has considerable support and reasoned arguments. A justified claim is a claim that has enough support to convince you (or us, or some body of opinion, or some ethnic group, or some nation) of its truth. This support may come in the form of information gained through our senses, opinions, memories, emotions, intuition, inner convictions, and so on. Often it is a combination of these. For example, if there were two candidates running for the position of mayor in my town, I might voice my opinion by citing Ms Patel's track record in politics, the high regard many people have for her, a memorable speech she made, and my intuitive preference for her. My friend may be a supporter of Loh Mei Lin, and she might justify her opinion in a similar way.

The point to note is that, although we both have opinions that are justified to our own satisfaction, our justifications do not prove anything one way or the other, and may not be enough to convince supporters of the other candidate. Our justifications simply mean that we both have reasons that are valid (at least to us) for thinking the way we do.

An unjustified opinion is one that is not based on good reasons. For example, if I said I thought Amandeep Patel would make a better leader because she is taller than Loh Mei Lin, my reason would not be valid (unless there was well-documented evidence to suggest taller people make better leaders), so my opinion would not be justified.

A similar argument can be put forward for justified beliefs. I may believe that William Shakespeare wrote *King Lear*. I can justify this belief by recalling that when I was at school I learnt that William Shakespeare wrote *King Lear*. In addition, I have read his name as playwright on every copy of the play I have ever seen, and, to the best of my knowledge, the play is attributed to him whenever it is performed.

King Lear was written well before I was born, so I did not witness Shakespeare writing this play or any other. I justify my belief on the grounds that most of the authorities I know of seem to accept William Shakespeare as the author. I have **valid reasons** for believing Shakespeare to have written *King Lear* and my belief could be regarded as justified.

However, suppose that in recent years I have become aware of a considerable number of people who strongly believe Shakespeare was not the author of all the works attributed to him. They cite a number of anomalies in the historical evidence to justify their beliefs. Is my belief in Shakespeare's authorship of *King Lear* still justified?

Compare the methods or procedures we use to justifying a knowledge claim within an area of knowledge (such as the natural sciences or history) with those we use to justify claims about knowledge.

- What are our underlying assumptions about these methods?

Think carefully about how you use words like think (as in voicing an opinion), believe and know when preparing your TOK assessments. How do you distinguish between an opinion, a belief, and a fact?

valid reason: a reason that is well-founded and convincing; a valid argument is an argument that follows the rules of logic

Task: think about

- What kind of social approval is needed for reasons to be regarded as valid?
- Can my belief that Shakespeare wrote *King Lear* really be justified if I have not carefully considered and weighed up the evidence against his authorship?

As we have seen, people on both sides of an argument can often justify their positions, so justification alone does not guarantee us knowledge. Sometimes, however, our justification is so convincing that we might declare a justified belief to be knowledge.

One example of this is the belief that the speed of light in a vacuum is 299,792,458 metres per second (also known as *c* for *constant*). Not everyone has the skills or the technical equipment to measure the speed of light in a vacuum, and relatively few people have even witnessed anyone else measuring it, but our belief about the speed of light is usually held on the grounds that all the scientific textbooks and websites we consult give us the same answer. In other words, we trust the knowledge of the various authorities we have consulted and we say that we know the speed of light in a vacuum is *c*.

What is evidence?

evidence: information that is interpreted to support a particular argument

We have already referred to **evidence** in our discussion about justification because justification often relies on evidence. By interpreting information in different ways, the same information can be used as evidence for or against different points of view.

An example of this is data showing prices rising on the stock market. One investor might take this trend as evidence for it being a good time to buy more shares. With prices rising, any shares she buys will appreciate in value and earn her a profit when she sells them. Another investor might look at the same data as evidence that the stock is too expensive to buy now. He may, on that basis, decide to wait until the stock market loses value before buying any shares, so that he can buy them at bargain prices.

The traditional nature of hunting can provide evidence for conflicting positions.

Another example might be the knowledge that Australian Aborigines traditionally hunt for their food. This information has been used to support the argument that they should be allowed to hunt in Australia's national parks because it is an essential aspect of their cultural heritage. Others have used the same information to support the argument that no-one should be allowed to hunt in national parks. Aboriginal hunting, they claim, was a contributory factor in the extinction of more than 60 species of mega-fauna including several species of giant kangaroos, and if Aboriginal hunting is allowed to continue in protected areas, even more species will be lost.

Because of the tremendous importance that evidence has in determining what is accepted as knowledge, some areas of knowledge have rules about what can and what cannot be evidence. This is particularly true in a court of law. For example, physical evidence must be collected in a particular way that makes it as free from contamination as possible. Statements made under torture cannot be admitted as evidence, and opinions can only be accepted from 'expert' witnesses.

When we have enough evidence to be able to claim something as true, we may view this as **proof** of its truth. How much evidence is enough will vary from subject to subject, and will also depend on the context. If chicken sausages go missing from a shop and, soon after, the butcher sees a dog running down the road with sausages in its mouth, the butcher may regard this as 'proof' that the dog has stolen the sausages. But is it really enough evidence to convict the dog? Can you think of other explanations?

Evidence in science

In science, **anecdotal evidence** is not usually admitted because it is not based on a scientific study. It can be very unreliable and the results cannot be tested.

For example, I might say I know a person who cured his eczema by eating papaya every day. This story may be based upon two correct observations: I know a person who had eczema, and that person's eczema went away after he had eaten papaya daily. But eczema sometimes goes away spontaneously. How can anyone be sure it was the papaya that cured him? Perhaps it wasn't the papaya but the lime juice or cinnamon he sprinkled on it that helped. Or maybe the eczema had been an allergic reaction to pineapple, and he stopped eating pineapple when he started to eat papaya. Or perhaps there was a change in humidity about the time he started eating papaya, and that is what made the difference.

As we can see, there are lots of different ways in which the disappearance of the eczema might be explained. This example illustrates the familiar scientific principle that neither **coincidence** nor **correlation** implies **causation**.

In Chapter 6 we will discuss the scientific method in some detail. In this chapter it is enough to say that some scientific evidence comes from observations and measurements made in experiments using the scientific method. For example, the evidence for **Newton's Law of Gravitation** comes from data taken from many experiments. Other evidence is drawn from observations of the world and the universe, but these observations must be made according to scientific guidelines if they are to be taken seriously. If observations are not carefully documented and reviewed, or if they do not fit with an accepted body of scientific knowledge, then they may be discounted or even dismissed by scientists who are weighing up evidence.

proof: enough evidence to claim something as true

Do not use the words 'evidence' and 'proof' interchangeably. They do *not* mean the same thing. Similarly, do not say your evidence 'proves' your thesis when you really mean that your evidence 'supports' it.

anecdotal evidence: evidence that comes from personal stories

coincidence: when two or more events happen at the same time independently of each other

correlation: when there is a relationship between two or more events, but it is not necessarily a causal relationship

causation: when one event leads to another event, for example kicking a football causes the ball to move

Newton's Law of Gravitation
Every particle of matter in the universe attracts every other particle with a force that is directly proportional to the product of the masses of the particles and inversely proportional to the square of the distance between them.

What is the significance of key points in the historical development of knowledge? Think about the following:

- How has our understanding of what constitutes knowledge or evidence developed over time?

Real-life situation

For many years the tobacco industry tried to hide the fact that smoking causes cancer by appealing to the lack of evidence of a causal link, on the grounds that correlation doesn't imply causation.

- How much evidence should there be, and what kind of evidence do we need, before we are prepared to accept there is a causal link between two events?

Evidence in history

In history, evidence may come in the form of buildings, artefacts, geographical features, different types of documents, photographs and artworks, eyewitness testimonies, and so on. Sometimes historians will view certain evidence as unreliable. For example, an eyewitness statement may be very biased and therefore not give an accurate account of the event witnessed. Usually historians will still consider the account as evidence, but may decide not to give too much weight to it. In some cases, however, there may be little choice: there may be only one existing account of an event, and the historian needs to make a judgement about the extent to which the account can be relied on.

When studying artefacts, historians have to consider and interpret the circumstances in which an artefact is found. For example, a recent discovery of Roman coins in Anuvanahalli (a place in India where traditionally many medicinal plants have been grown), along with some stone weights of different sizes, has led historians to believe the site may have been used as a centre for preparing herbal medicines to sell to the Romans.

Ancient coins provide important clues for historians.

Task: think about

Imagine that two first-century Roman coins were found in Antarctica. How convinced would you be that the coins were evidence that the Romans had traded with people in Antarctica?

Evidence in the arts

It is very difficult to come to grips with evidence in the arts. We all have preferences in terms of music, drama and visual arts. Often these preferences are cultural: we tend to like the art, music and dramas that are familiar to us, or that are enjoyed by our peers. But can we say one performance is better than another, or one particular artwork is superior to another?

We may compare the arts in terms of technical difficulties, but even this is problematic. It may be easy, for example, to judge that greater skill is needed to play Chopin's Etude Op. 25 No. 10 than to play *Chopsticks* on a piano. But can we judge the skill differential between playing Beethoven's *Für Elise* and Jimmy Hendrix's *Purple Haze*?

Some people would argue that our appreciation of the arts is entirely relative; there is no way we can claim one piece of work to be better than another. However, IB students studying music, visual arts, film, dance or theatre will have their work assessed. An examiner will have to decide what grade their work is worthy of, and this grade will need to be justified on the basis of evidence. This evidence may include assessments of aspects of the work such as the performer's technical skills, understanding of techniques, exploration and development of ideas, and creativeness.

Task: activity

Look at Wassily Kandinsky's *Cossacks* and Mark Rothko's *Light Red over Black* on the internet. Is it possible to judge which artwork shows more creativity? What sort of criteria would you use to decide?

Task: think about

- To what extent do we have to know an artist's intentions to appreciate an artwork?
- How important are the views of 'experts' in evaluating the relative merits of art, dance, drama and music?

Art galleries and collectors are often prepared to pay many millions of dollars for a particular work of art yet regard a well-made forgery of the same work as relatively worthless even if it may have fooled experts for years. The value cannot be in the aesthetics because both the masterpiece and the master-forgery may be identical to look at, and the differences may only be discernable under intense technical scrutiny.

This raises two questions about evidence in the arts. What kind of evidence do we have to assure us that *Girl with a Pearl Earring* in the Mauritshuis Gallery in The Hague was really painted by Johannes Vermeer? And what evidence do we have that this painting has greater artistic merit than my pretty painting of a girl with a necklace?

The answer to the first of these questions is relatively easy. Carbon dating, chemical analysis of paints and canvas, X-rays, careful study by experts of techniques, and the **provenance** of the artwork are important contributions to the body of evidence that supports or rejects an artwork's claim to be 'an original'. What is not so easy is the answer to the second question.

> **provenance**: a record of ownership, ideally going back to the artist in the case of an artwork

One possible answer is that people are prepared to pay many millions of dollars for the Vermeer, but not for my painting. But is the willingness of people to pay money really evidence of greater artistic merit? If so, why did Vincent van Gogh die a pauper? The public of his time may not have valued his work, but today his paintings are priceless. Willingness to spend money on something possibly says more about the purchasers than it does about the products purchased: someone once bid $15,000 for an air guitar on eBay (an air guitar is an imaginary guitar that people pretend to play).

Task: think about

- If even experts cannot tell a genuine Rembrandt from a forgery, why is a forgery worth so much less when it is revealed as a forgery?
- It is currently estimated that 10–40% of artworks for sale that are reputedly created by important artists are forgeries, and at least 20% of artworks owned by museums are misattributed. If this estimate is correct, how might art galleries be *justified* in paying large sums of public money for famous works of art?

Real-life situation

Tom Keating was an art forger and restorer who is said to have forged thousands of works of more than 100 different artists including Rembrandt. He regarded his forgeries as a stand against corruption and shallowness in the world of art, and he used them to fool the art experts of his time. Since his death his forgeries have become collectors' pieces in their own right and sell for high prices at auctions, although not as much as the originals that he copied.

- If two artists create identical pictures of the same subject, on what grounds is one painting worth more than the other?
- How does a society decide which artists to respect and which to ignore?

Tom Keating, art forger, at work.

Knowledge questions

- To what extent do we evaluate evidence before making a judgement, and to what extent do we look for evidence to support our judgements?
- How does the importance of justifying our beliefs differ across different areas of knowledge?

Presentation task

Choose one of the knowledge questions above. Consider how you might develop it for a presentation. Select some real-life examples that you might use as evidence to support and to counter your argument.

Extended writing task

Write 500 words on one of the following questions:

1 To what extent are we persuaded by the quantity of evidence rather than the quality of evidence?

2 How can we justify beliefs that do not seem to agree with available evidence?

3 To what extent can we justify beliefs that rest on very flimsy or anecdotal evidence? And why might we want to hold or justify such beliefs?

Prescribed essay titles

1 'The knowledge that we value the most is the knowledge for which we can provide the strongest justifications.' To what extent would you agree with this claim? (November 2008 and May 2009)

2 'Doubt is the key to knowledge.' (Persian proverb) To what extent is this true in two areas of knowledge? (November 2010 and May 2011)

3 To what extent do we need evidence to support our beliefs in different areas of knowledge? (November 2010 and May 2011)

Further reading and sources

Gladwell, Malcolm. 2006. *Blink: The Power of Thinking Without Thinking*. Penguin.

Glover, Michael. '*The big question: How many of the paintings in our public museums are fakes?*' The Independent, 16 April 2010. Available at: www.independent.co.uk/artsentertainment/art/news/the-big-question-how-many-of-the-paintings-in-our-publicmuseums-are-fakes-1946264.html

Landesman, Peter. '*A 20th-century master scam*', The New York Times Magazine. Available at: www.nytimes.com/library/magazine/archive/19990718mag-art-forger.html

Twelve Angry Men DVD (1957) based on a playscript written by Reginald Rose in 1955.

3 Shared and personal knowledge

Introduction

So far we have discussed what we mean by knowledge, and we have considered some of the evidence we might call upon to justify calling a belief 'knowledge'. You may have noticed that in the process we must often rely on a social consensus to validate our evidence and our knowledge claims.

In Chapter 1, we categorised knowledge into practical knowledge, knowledge by acquaintance and factual knowledge. Although these are very useful ways of considering what knowledge is, this division is not the only way that knowledge can be broken down. In this chapter we will look at shared and personal knowledge.

As the knower is central to TOK, personal knowledge is important, but your work in TOK must reflect a balance between your personal knowledge and shared knowledge in the areas of knowledge you consider. Often this will not be a 50/50 balance because what we know usually depends far more on shared knowledge than what we have learnt through personal experience or acquaintance.

Shared knowledge

shared knowledge: what we know as part of a group or community; for example, what we learn through the curriculum at school is a set of skills and information agreed on by educators, politicians and others as important knowledge for our society

Simply put, we might want to state that **shared knowledge** is knowledge that is shared by a group, for example a family, ethnic group, religious faction, company or language community. In some cases, shared knowledge might even be global: for example, most people in the world may know that Washington D.C. is the capital of the United States of America. Shared knowledge can include all three of our categories from Chapter 1: a culture may share practical knowledge in the form of cooking techniques or art; an ethnic group may share knowledge by acquaintance of their habitat; a society may share factual knowledge about its history.

In each of these cases, although not every single member of the culture, ethnic group or society may 'know' the shared knowledge, the majority of the group are aware of the knowledge and affirm it as true. Those who do not affirm the knowledge as true might say they know *about* their society's beliefs, but may not regard them as knowledge.

We often rely upon shared knowledge for affirmation or refutation of our personal beliefs and opinions. For example, if I believe in ghosts, this belief is likely to be reinforced if the society I live in 'knows' ghosts exist, that is to say, if the society I live in regards the existence of ghosts as a fact. But if I live in a society that 'knows' ghosts are imaginary, I might give up my belief in ghosts. The shared knowledge interacts with my personal knowledge largely through the roles played by language and education, both of which are socially constructed.

Task: think about

- Can we claim a group 'knows' something if not everyone in that group agrees?
- If every member of a group is in agreement, does that make what is agreed upon a 'fact'?
- How do those in authority decide which knowledge is to be shared through education, and how do their decisions shape our shared knowledge?

The shared knowledge discussed so far is not the only type of shared knowledge. There is some knowledge that we share as a society, a nation or a world that few individuals have any detailed knowledge of. For example, many countries have an automobile industry that manufactures cars. We could say that the Japanese know how to make cars, but few people from any country have the knowledge to make a car from scratch on their own; even nations depend on other nations for some of the parts and technology they use.

This type of shared knowledge is better known as **distributed knowledge**, which is the combined knowledge of all the individuals in a society. The more complex and knowledgeable a society or an organisation becomes, the more it must rely on distributed knowledge. No-one can know everything there is to know, and we must often call on experts for their skills or advice. Each area of knowledge has its own subject specialists, and often these areas are themselves broken down into sub-specialisms. For example, if you go to see your medical doctor about a sore eye, you may be referred to an ophthalmologist who specialises in eye problems.

Distributed knowledge is one of the reasons why classroom discussions are so important. Often people can have knowledge that, on its own, may seem insignificant, but, when pooled with the knowledge of others, can be of immense

distributed knowledge: the combined knowledge of all the individuals in an organisation, society, nation or the world

How do social networking sites embody distributed knowledge?

value. To maximise learning in a classroom it is important that everyone is a learner and everyone is a teacher, and that students do not sit passively, expecting to learn all the information they need from the teacher who is leading the class.

> **Task: think about**
>
> - What things can you do or what things do you know that do not rely on skills or knowledge learned from other people?
> - How do social networking sites embody distributed knowledge?

Compare the implications of shared knowledge for individual perspectives in different areas of knowledge.

We could argue that shared knowledge is the most important type of knowledge. We live in societies, and societies can only function because of the knowledge that is shared across them. All of our laws, books, and scientific, academic, medical and technical expertise depend on shared knowledge. This knowledge is drawn from the experiences of many people across the world's history. However important our personal knowledge may be to us, it can only contribute to the world's wealth of knowledge when it is shared with others.

> **Real-life situation**
>
> Singularity University is an organisation in NASA Research Park, Silicon Valley. Its aim is to mix some of the world's most brilliant entrepreneurs and leaders with some of the world's most creative technologists and thinkers in a collaborative environment where they can turn their attention to addressing the greatest challenges facing humankind.
>
> - Why does Singularity University not just bring medical specialists together to solve medical problems, or agriculturalists together to solve food problems, or computer specialists together to solve technology problems?
> - What are the advantages and disadvantages of a collaborative approach?

Personal knowledge

No amount of reading about hunger will help me to know what it is; I will only know what it feels like when I have experienced the gnawing sensation myself. Similarly, if I say I know John Lennon's *Imagine* I mean that I am familiar with the music, the lyrics, or both. If I have merely heard of the song, I may say I 'know of' it but I would not be able to say that I 'know' it.

Much of what we learn as young babies is knowledge by acquaintance that we gain through personal experience as we explore our environment. Basic knowledge such as what is food and what is not, who are our care-givers, and how to manipulate objects with our hands, is all learnt through our early experiences of the world, and forms part of our **personal knowledge**.

Sometimes we know something without fully understanding it. For example, we may know that the relationship between the rotation, orbit and angle of inclination of the axis of the Earth causes the differences in the seasons and hours of daylight in different places, but we may not understand the details. We 'know about' these things without understanding them and without having a deeper personal knowledge of them.

Of course personal knowledge may also be shared. For example, I may know from experience that bread can be eaten, and this is knowledge shared by most

personal knowledge: the knowledge we have through our own experiences and personal involvement; this can include knowledge by acquaintance, practical knowledge and factual knowledge

people around the world. Or I may know how to speak Russian. The knowledge I have of the Russian language is personal, but this knowledge is only possible because of the *shared* nature of language.

Task: think about

I may not know from personal experience that witchetty grubs can be eaten, but I may know this through being familiar with some aspects of Australian Aboriginal culture.

- Is my knowledge that witchetty grubs are edible knowledge by acquaintance?
- Is it personal or shared knowledge?

Tacit knowledge

A great deal of our personal knowledge is **tacit**, that is, knowledge that cannot easily be communicated to others. To take an extreme example, Rachmaninov is widely regarded to have been one of the greatest pianists ever. We might say that it was the subtlety of his finger technique that made him better than other concert pianists who can read the same music and play the same notes. But while we might be able to explain what we mean by finger technique, we are not able to explain to anyone how they can play like Rachmaninov did. Only Rachmaninov knew how to play like Rachmaninov, and even then he only knew it tacitly.

In cricket, all batsmen are taught to 'watch the ball', but what is it that Sachin Tendulkar knows that enables him to see so much more than other batsmen? No matter how many talented cricketers he coaches, he cannot pass on his tacit knowledge.

All of us have tacit knowledge. We may know how to play the guitar or we may recognise the voice of Priyanka Chopra in a commercial voiceover, but we may not be able to explain to anyone else how we do either of these. We may be able to say how we have come to have this knowledge (by having guitar lessons for many years or having watched several of Priyanka Chopra's movies) but not *what it is that we know* other than at a very superficial level.

> **tacit**: understood or implied without being explicitly stated

If you had a horse you might be able to recognise him among others that are similar, but could you describe him to someone else so that they could recognise him?

Tacit knowledge may be shared in the sense that others may share tacit abilities that we have, such as how to recognise familiar faces. Tacit knowledge can also be shared in the distributed sense. For example, the medical profession has the ability to perform organ transplants, but to carry out such surgery requires a team of people each with specialised knowledge. Some of the skills of the surgeon, the anaesthetist and others will often fall into the category of tacit knowledge and will also form an integral part of the distributed knowledge of the surgical team.

> **Task: think about**
>
> - Can you describe a person or an animal you know well in such a way that someone who does not know them would recognise them from a group with similar characteristics?
> - Other than the ability to recognise friends and family, what other tacit knowledge do you have?
> - Which ways of knowing are most closely linked with tacit knowledge?

> **Task: think about**
>
> Suppose I am a great fan of the veteran pop star Cliff Richard. I may own every record he has ever made, I may have been to many of his concerts and read every book about him. I can probably answer most questions about him where the answers are a matter of public knowledge. My friend Ho is also a Cliff Richard fan but owns only two of his records, has never read a book about him and knows very few details about his life. Ho, however, has met Sir Cliff socially on a number of occasions, and they have had several long conversations.
>
> - Which of us can claim to know Cliff Richard? What do we mean by *know* in this case?
> - Suppose someone has met and spoken with Helen Clark (an ex-prime minister of New Zealand) on two separate occasions, but cannot recall many of the details of those meetings. Can he or she claim to *know* Helen Clark?
> - What are the expectations we have if one person claims to *know* another?

Compare the responsibilities of individuals who have expert tacit knowledge in different areas of knowledge. Think about the following:

- How does tacit knowledge in the arts differ from tacit knowledge in mathematics and the natural sciences?

In his book *The Tacit Dimension*, Michael Polanyi reconsidered human knowledge starting with 'we can know more than we can tell'.

In his influential book *Personal Knowledge*, Michael Polanyi argues that all knowledge is at some level personal. He claims that each of us makes a decision about what evidence we accept and what we dismiss, what shared knowledge we adhere to and what we reject, and he includes scientific knowledge in this claim as well. Whatever we learn from our families, religious authorities, culture, schools, trusted printed or internet sources, or society, we must ultimately decide for ourselves what we will accept as knowledge. These decisions are inescapably personal.

Ways of knowing in shared and personal knowledge

We can think about the different ways of knowing in terms of their contribution to shared and personal knowledge. Many of the ways of knowing may seem predominantly personal, but it is through them that the immense body of shared knowledge is developed.

Language

Language is perhaps the most social of all ways of knowing. Languages evolve in different societies and cultures, and a language can only function as a means of communication as far as it is shared. If I create a new word (a *neologism*), it can only be embraced into the language and understood by other language users if I share what I mean by it. Without shared knowledge there could be no language, but how we hear and interpret language is also deeply personal.

> ### Task: think about
>
> Take the statement 'I don't like your haircut'. It sounds a simple statement. It contains no obscure words and, on one level, we all understand what it means because the words and the syntax are part of a shared vocabulary and a shared grammar. Yet how we interpret it can be very personal; it will very much depend on the context in which it is said, who is saying it and why.
>
> How might you understand it if it was said by:
> * your mother or father
> * your closest friend
> * your teacher
> * a 'school bully'
> * the hairdresser who gave you the haircut
> * a different hairdresser?

> Compare the role of language in different areas of knowledge. Think about the following:
> * How do personal word associations affect our understanding of different subject areas?

Emotion

Emotions are an intensely personal way of knowing. Emotions shape our thoughts and behaviours, and influence our interpretation of the world in a cyclical fashion. For example, reading positive words such as *confident, friendly, happy, successful* can increase our serotonin levels and make us feel happy and positive, whereas reading negative words like *miserable, sad, despondent, nervous* can contribute to a reduction in our serotonin levels and make us feel sad and less positive. These emotions will in turn affect the ways in which we respond to the circumstances we find ourselves in. Our emotions may ultimately determine how we interpret language and sense perceptions, how we respond to issues of faith, and how we apply our reason.

In ethical debates such as whether or not abortion, euthanasia or laboratory testing on animals should be legal, people on both sides of the arguments are frequently driven by their emotional responses to the issues and use emotive language to further their cause. Does this mean emotions are shared?

> Emotions are the subjective experiences of certain physical changes in our bodies. If these physical changes return to normal, the emotion disappears.

> ### Task: think about
>
> * Why do people often use emotive language in arguments?
> * To what extent do your emotions help you to learn something new? How well do you learn things that don't really interest you or excite your emotions?
> * If the rest of the class is excited about something, to what extent does this raise your levels of excitement?

Sensory perception

Our senses are what help us to understand the world around us, but our senses are only as good as our sensory apparatus and our brain's interpretation of the data it receives. Although we may see the same scene as others, the way in which we perceive it will be unique. The same can be said of music or conversations that we listen to, books that we read, foods that we taste, aromas that we smell, and so on. However public the source of our sense perception is, the awareness we have as a result of it will be individual and personal.

But our perceptions may still have much in common with the perceptions of others. Indeed, we often call upon others to confirm our sensory perceptions. We might ask our friends 'Did you see that?', 'Can you hear that noise?' or 'Does this milk smell off to you?' We are more likely to believe some of our sensory experiences if they seem to be shared by others.

> As well as hearing, vision, smell, taste and touch, we have many other senses including motion, equilibrium, pain and temperature.

Task: activity

The ability to 'fool' the brain is well known, and there are numerous optical illusions and interesting psychological experiments on the internet: for example, the rubber hand illusion, the Ames room and the McGurk effect. Try to look at some of them.

Task: think about

- How can the brain be fooled even when we know what the trick is?
- To what extent are our sensory perceptions shaped by the reported sense perceptions of others?
- To what extent can sensory perceptions be shared?

Imagination

'Imagination is more important than knowledge. For knowledge is limited, whereas imagination embraces the entire world, stimulating progress, giving birth to evolution. It is, strictly speaking, a real factor in scientific research.'

Albert Einstein

Mostly when we talk about imagination we are referring to ideas and images 'in our head' but, as we shall see, imagination can play an important role in knowing in areas as diverse as the arts, history and mathematics. In the arts, imagination can lead the way to the creation of something new; in history, imagination can weave a story that connects isolated ideas and help to create a coherent whole; in mathematics, imagination enables us to create and manipulate multi-dimensional spaces which can lead mathematicians to new ideas and solutions.

In each of these areas, what may begin in an individual's imagination can lead to shared knowledge.

Our sensory perception is often informed by our imagination.

Task: think about

Albert Einstein is perhaps the most celebrated of all physicists and was one of the world's most creative minds. He was a great advocate of imagination as a way to making scientific progress, and yet science is more typically associated with reason.

- Why do you think some people are reluctant to acknowledge the role of imagination in science?
- To what extent must imagination be shared if it is to lead to shared knowledge?

Intuition

'A new idea comes suddenly and in a rather intuitive way. But intuition is nothing but the outcome of earlier intellectual experience.'

Albert Einstein

Intuition is a way of knowing without relying on reasons or justifications. Many psychologists regard it as immediate ideas that are subconsciously based upon previous knowledge and experience. We could say that it is grounded in tacit knowledge.

Intuition is frequently used in mathematics and in science to find a way to a solution. It may guide us in terms of who or what we choose to trust in many areas of knowledge. In their book *Meaning*, Michael Polanyi and Harry Prosch make the point that intuition is the name we give to things the brain knows that we do not know we know; it is similar to going to sleep with a problem in your head and waking up with a solution, having given it no conscious thought in the meantime.

Task: think about

- In what circumstances do you trust your intuition?
- How far can you trust your intuition?

Memory

We cannot know anything without memory. We cannot even claim to know what we are experiencing at the present, because our present experiences are understood in the context of past experiences and knowledge. How would you read this book if you couldn't remember what the words meant? Indeed, how would you know it was a book? Memory can be very personal – only you have immediate access to your memories – but shared memories are essential to our societies. Our collective memories of present and past generations are available to us all through books, journals, folklore, and so on, and it is these memories that allow us to build on the knowledge and achievements of others.

Task: think about

- To what extent could there be culture, science, religion, mathematics, ethics, arts, human sciences or indigenous knowledge without shared memories?
- What is the difference between a personal memory of an experience and a shared memory written in a book?

Faith

Most of what we know we accept on trust. If you are doing research for a project or for your Extended Essay, you may read books, journals, newspapers, websites, and so on for information. If you learn, write down and use information you find, you are taking it on faith that the authors of those different sources have been honest and accurate in what they have written. Books and journals from reputable publishers tend to be more reliable than self-published works, which is why we need to be extra cautious when taking information from the internet.

We take on faith things told to us by our friends, our family, our teachers and 'experts'. If, for example, a dentist tells us we need a filling, we usually take it on faith that she has the knowledge and experience to know what work needs doing,

The internet gives us ready access to sites that have excellent information, but it also gives us ready access to sites that have erroneous information, and it is not always easy to tell a good site from a poor one. Even publications from respected publishers can contain errors so it is good practice to consult a range of sources when seeking information for any of your essays or assignments.

and enough professional integrity not to give us wrong advice. If we doubt the dentist's knowledge or integrity we may seek a second, independent opinion.

We also take on faith our religious and cultural beliefs. Usually these are aspects of our world that we learn from our families and our communities, in the same way that we learn most of the basic knowledge and skills we need for survival. They are often deeply ingrained in us because we learn them from early childhood.

Faith is essential for us to live our everyday lives. Even when we buy items from the shops we take it on faith that what we have bought meets the claims that are made 'on the tin'. Sometimes our lives may depend upon that faith. For example, if we suffer from a severe gluten allergy and we buy bread labelled 'gluten-free', we take it on faith that there was no wheat used in making the bread. If we get into a taxi or a tuk-tuk and ask the driver to take us somewhere, we are placing our faith in the driver and his vehicle to take us safely where we want to go. When Jean-François Gravelet, better known as Blondin, proposed walking a tightrope across Niagara Falls, blindfolded and pushing a wheelbarrow, many people may have believed he was capable of it, but it was the woman who agreed to sit in the wheelbarrow who demonstrated her faith.

What are the implications of shared knowledge accepted by faith for our individual perspectives?

What assumptions underlie our personal approach to shared knowledge?

Jean-François Gravelet walking a tightrope across Niagara Falls.

Even science must rely upon faith. If scientists did not share faith in a rational and orderly universe, scientific observations and experiments would be meaningless. So far their faith in a rational and orderly universe appears to be justified, but we have only explored a very small fraction of it in time and space.

Task: think about

- Not all cultures believe in a rational and orderly universe. How might our lives be different if we did not share scientists' belief in a rational universe?
- To what extent does our opinion about whom or what we may place our faith in depend on how many others share that opinion?
- When it comes to accepting knowledge by faith, are we influenced more by who shares that knowledge or *how many others* share that knowledge?

Reason

'Reason is, and ought only to be the slave of the passions, and can never pretend to any other office than to serve and obey them.'

David Hume

Reason is often thought to be a defining characteristic of what it is to be human. However, like so many key words associated with knowledge, there are many philosophical debates about what reason is. There are several different types of reasoning, some of which will be introduced in this book; what is important is that all of them are *shared*. That is to say, there are socially accepted definitions of what constitutes reason and what does not.

Everything we do in TOK is related to reason in one way or another. When we construct an argument or justify a belief, we are using reason. We even use reason to assess our intuition and imagination. Some of our ideas about what constitutes reason are shared. For example, there is a general agreement by mathematicians, philosophers and logicians about what is valid reasoning and what is not in formal logic. But formal logic (deductive reasoning) can never lead to certainty except in so far as the **premises** it starts with are certain, and other forms of reasoning such as inductive reasoning are inherently fallible.

That said, it is popularly believed that reason is the ultimate way of knowing. When we examine a knowledge claim we ask ourselves whether the claim is *reasonable*. When we write essays for the IB, the assessment criteria include whether we can make coherent and compelling arguments. An argument in this sense is the ability to persuade using reason and evidence. The requirement that our arguments be *reasonable* is one that is widely shared.

> **premise**: a proposition assumed to be true, on which an argument is based

> Are there limitations to the use of reason as a way of knowing in different areas of knowledge?

Task: think about

- What do you think the philosopher David Hume meant when he said reason is 'the slave of the passions'?
- Why do you think people tend to associate faith with religion and reason with science? Are those associations *reasonable*?
- Does shared knowledge rely on reason more than personal knowledge?

Real-life situation

During a game of football we see examples of tacit personal knowledge in the individual skills of the players and referee, distributed knowledge in the distributed skills of the teams and officials, and shared knowledge of the strategies and rules of the game.

- Is any one form of knowledge more important in football or any other team sport?
- What about in an operating theatre, or in an orchestra?

Knowledge questions

- How do shared and personal knowledge complement each other?
- To what extent is all knowledge personal?
- Can something be called *knowledge* if it is not shared?

Presentation task

Consider how you might develop the first knowledge question for a presentation. What real-life situations might your developed questions apply to?

Extended writing task

Write 500 words on one or both of the following questions:

1 How do we decide which knowledge claims to trust when our personal knowledge is at odds with knowledge that is widely shared?

2 When, if ever, should society allow personal knowledge claims to change shared knowledge?

Prescribed essay titles

1 In areas of knowledge such as the arts and the sciences, do we learn more from work that follows or that breaks with accepted conventions? (November 2007 and May 2008)

2 How important are the opinions of experts in the search for knowledge? (November 2010 and May 2011)

3 To understand something you need to rely on your own experience and culture. Does this mean that it is impossible to have objective knowledge? (November 2008 and May 2009)

Further reading and sources

Isaacson, Walter. 2007. *Einstein: His Life and Universe*. Simon & Schuster.
Polanyi, Michael. 1958. *Personal Knowledge: Towards a Post-Critical Philosophy*. Routledge & Paul Kegan.
Polanyi, Michael. 1966. *The Tacit Dimension*. Doubleday.
Polanyi, Michael and Prosch, Harry. 1975. *Meaning*. University of Chicago Press.
Winston, Robert. 2004. *The Human Mind*. Random House.

4 Knowledge frameworks and ways of knowing

Introduction

The IB recommends that you study *six* out of the *eight* areas of knowledge: mathematics, science, human science, history, the arts, ethics, religious knowledge systems and indigenous knowledge systems. These eight areas of knowledge are the subjects of the remaining chapters of this unit.

Unit 2 sets out to explore the knowledge framework. The knowledge framework is a *tool for analysis and comparison* between different areas of knowledge. The purpose of the knowledge framework is to help you think 'across' areas of knowledge. There are five interacting parts to the knowledge framework: (1) scope, motivation and applications, (2) specific terminology and concepts, (3) methods used to produce knowledge, (4) key historical developments and (5) interaction with personal knowledge. The knowledge framework is like a *map* to help you find your way and develop your sense of the connections between areas of knowledge. Identifying and exploring the similarities and differences between areas of knowledge is one type of TOK analysis.

In Chapters 5–12 of this unit, there are notes in the margin to help you make connections and links with the framework. These are intended only to support and guide you; they are no substitute for your own critical thought, ideas and analysis.

Think about the links and connections between different areas of knowledge.

- In what ways are two areas of knowledge similar?
- In what ways are these two areas different?

What counts as a fact? What counts as an explanation? What is a reliable method for gaining knowledge? Each area of knowledge has its own answers to these questions.

The structure and conventions of an area of knowledge can be divided up into a 'knowledge framework'. The purpose of a knowledge framework is to make it easier to compare the similarities and differences between two or more areas of knowledge.

Like a map, knowledge is a representation of the world. Each area of knowledge can be divided into at least five different parts. This is called a knowledge framework. Like a map, the framework helps you find your way around different areas of knowledge and make connections and links between them.

The knowledge framework

Part 1: Scope and applications

scope: the subject content
of an area of knowledge

The first part of the framework invites you to explore what each area of knowledge is about, what defines our shared knowledge, and what problems it addresses. **Scope** is to do with the subject matter or the area of knowledge. Mathematics is about ideas such as shape, number and pattern. Ethics is about moral choices. The topics studied as part of the history curriculum may be thought of as the subject content of history; however, the 'history' area of knowledge itself is very much broader than this. You might think critically about the factors that shape our impression of subject matter: our personal experience of the subject, the IB curriculum, our culture, our type of education. Subject matter is also related to the problems that an area of knowledge deals with.

applications: how
knowledge is used, whether it
is to identify problems or find
solutions

- When is it ethically wrong
  to pursue knowledge?
  When is it wrong to use
  knowledge? When is it
  right?
- In what ways might
  these sorts of ethical
  considerations shape the
  scope and applications of
  an area of knowledge?

Applications refer to the practical problems and solutions the area of knowledge addresses. In mathematics, we can address real-world problems such as the probability of a ball landing on a certain number on a roulette wheel. Different fields of science and technology have different applications. If we are faced with a moral dilemma, where we are undecided between two courses of action, ethics might help us decide on what the better course of action is.

Task: activity

1 Can you think of any examples of the scope of two areas of knowledge, such as history and science? Compare the two areas of knowledge by making two lists, outlining examples of the different subject matter of each.
2 Can you think of any examples of the *practical problems and solutions* that two areas of knowledge, such as history and science, seek to answer? Compare the areas of knowledge by making two new lists with two headings, *the scope of history* and *the scope of science*, outlining examples of problems and solutions.
3 In what ways do you think your impression of the *scope* of an area of knowledge is influenced by your educational curriculum, your cultural context, your ethical values or any other factors?

Part 2: Specific terminology and concepts

language: to do with
words and communication

key concepts: the ideas that
form the basis of the area of
knowledge

The second part of the framework invites you again to look 'across' different areas of shared knowledge by identifying **language** and **key concepts**. Language enables knowledge to be communicated across cultures and forward to future generations. It enables us to build on the knowledge handed down to us. In some subject areas, language itself can count as knowledge. The purpose of this part of the framework is to identify the *similarities and differences* between concepts in different areas of knowledge.

This part of the knowledge
framework invites you to think
about how what counts as
knowledge is shaped by concepts
and language. In what ways do
language and concepts lead to
similarity and difference between
areas of knowledge?

- In history, the recorded past is studied using the concepts of evidence, reliability, causation, interpretation and accuracy.
- The study of the natural world in the sciences uses the concepts of hypothesis, inductive reasoning, experiment and scientific theory.
- In ethics, an action can be considered in relation to a number of key concepts, including right and wrong, intention, duty and consequence.
- In the arts, the key concepts include creativity, form, genre, style, texture, shape, colour, tempo and language.

1 Pick a particular concept, such as evidence, hypothesis or theory. Think of examples of how that concept is used to gain knowledge in different areas, such as history or human science.
2 Choose a particular area of knowledge and try to identify the key concepts that belong to it.
3 Give examples of how our language and concepts shape what we know in this area of knowledge.

Part 3: Methods used to produce knowledge

The third part of the knowledge framework invites you to think about the **methods** used to gain knowledge in each area of knowledge. This is to do with the procedure and process for gaining knowledge in a particular subject area, which varies for each area of knowledge.

- For example, both science and history make use of hypotheses and require data or evidence. The scientific method involves the formation of hypotheses which are tested by performing experiments. Historians use an empirical method based on interpretation of primary and secondary sources.
- Different methods used will lead to different knowledge claims and explanations. A historical fact could include the date of an event, whereas an explanation of a historical event would involve an understanding of its causes.

methods: the procedures and processes used to gain knowledge. Quantitative methods include statistical analysis, mathematical modelling, and laboratory experiments. Qualitative methods might include observation, interviews, questionnaires and case studies.

1 Give examples of *facts* from two or more areas of knowledge.
2 Give examples of *explanations* from two or more areas of knowledge.
3 Briefly explain the *methods* that can be used to generate these facts and explanations.

Part 4: Key historical developments

Our subject knowledge is a result of its historical and cultural context. If you look back to an encyclopedia from a century ago you can appreciate that what we take for granted now as shared knowledge is radically different from what it was in the past.

History is an area of knowledge as well as a part of the knowledge framework. This part of the framework invites you to think about how an area of knowledge has developed over time. How has history shaped the area of knowledge that we know today? Tracing the historical development of an area of knowledge can be a tool for analysis. If you ask the counterfactual question 'What if *x* had not happened?' you can speculate about how our knowledge might be partly the product of 'accidents of history'.

For example, if the discovery of chemical elements had not been made in chemistry, we would not have the Periodic Table that we know today. Without the discovery of DNA, the study of biology would be very different. And our knowledge in physics would be radically different without the discovery of quantum mechanics or the Higgs boson particle.

In this part of the knowledge framework you might also look at how the ways of knowing have developed over time: for example, the history of reason and rationality in the West, the Middle East or Asia; or the history of faith. An awareness of the intellectual movements of history such as the Renaissance and the Enlightenment can help us appreciate how science and rationality have led to a modern understanding of our place in the universe.

New concepts and ideas emerge and shape what we come to know. Given that our knowledge changes and develops over time, consider how far our knowledge is a product of history.

- How far is it shaped by other factors such as social convention, conformity and authority?
- To what extent is your own knowledge one of many other possible perspectives?

Part 5: Links with personal knowledge

The first four parts of the framework concern shared knowledge; the last part is to do with how that shared knowledge interacts with your own personal knowledge. This is the one part of the framework that is unique in relation to the other four parts, as it concerns you directly.

Personal knowledge is what 'I know' personally, and shared knowledge is what 'we know', together as a school community, or a local community, or as a nation or as an international community. The interaction between personal and shared knowledge can work in at least two ways.

Firstly, you as an individual can contribute to shared knowledge. For example, if you went on to do a postgraduate research degree at university this could lead to a discovery of new knowledge. Secondly, your own personal knowledge is shaped by the shared knowledge you have been brought up with. For example, most people believe that the Earth is about 4.5 billion years old, unless of course, they are creation scientists or their supporters, or hold a different scientific viewpoint.

Shared knowledge has an impact on what you as an individual know. A student's personal knowledge of their place in the world is affected by the shared knowledge that scientists tell us about how relatively short our time on the planet has been.

Ways of knowing

The IB recommends that you study *four* of the *eight* ways of knowing: reason, emotion, faith, imagination, sense perception, intuition, language and memory.

The main question in TOK is 'how do I know?' or 'how do we know?' Ways of knowing can give you a personal or shared answer to this question. We can claim to know something because we use rationality (reason), because we feel something (emotion), because we can think creatively (imagination), or because we have the labels and words (language) to describe it. There are many links between these ways of knowing. When you solve a mathematics problem you may be relying on your sense perception, reason and imagination. The following brief summaries do not provide a full explanation of each way of knowing; they are intended to start you thinking. The ways of knowing are explored in more detail in the later chapters of Unit 2.

Language

Language is a way of knowing as well as being the second part of the knowledge framework. Language is universal. In its broadest sense, language is to do with our intended communication, words, sounds and gestures. Language is a way to communicate our knowledge between individuals, and pass it between different cultures and onwards to the next generation. Animals also have a complex way of communicating and you might wonder what makes our speech distinct from a dog barking or a monkey shrieking. The language we use communicates our values: one person's 'terrorist' is another person's 'freedom fighter'. The Sapir–Whorf hypothesis, named after the American linguists Edward Sapir and Benjamin Lee Whorf, suggests that language does more than communicate our knowledge: it determines the way we think. Is our knowledge shaped by language? Does language function to communicate our knowledge? These are debates to explore. Can we know something without the words or language to express it? If we are articulate and fluent, are we regarded as knowledgeable? How does language connect with our emotions, imagination and memory?

Think of the ways of knowing as knowledge tools. Just as we need different tools for different practical tasks, we need to use different ways of knowing and different methods to gain knowledge.

Reason

The history of reason and rational thought is something you might explore in Part 4 of the knowledge framework. For example, you could explore the history of reason and the concept of *dharma* in Indian traditions from the Vedas to the present day, or the development of reason during the Islamic civilisation of the tenth to the twelfth century CE.

It is important to make distinctions between rationality, reasoning and good reasons. Our culture may influence how we think of rationality and reason. For example, reasoning in Aboriginal culture can be compared with other cultural perspectives. **Inductive reasoning** begins with particular observations and reasons to general conclusions. For example, my particular experiment observations that magnesium appears to increase its mass when it is burnt could lead me to the general conclusion that 'all magnesium appears to increase its mass when burnt'. **Deductive reasoning** begins with true premises and a valid argument to reach a conclusion that is also true. Rationality plays a key role in mathematics and science but might also extend to how we judge art or how we arrive at ethical decisions. What are its strengths and weaknesses as a way of knowing? Is reason a superior way of knowing? How does reason connect with emotion and faith? Is it a reliable source of knowledge?

inductive reasoning: moves from particular observations, experiences, or data to general conclusions

deductive reasoning: moves from the general to the particular

Emotion

Our feelings can be regarded as either an obstacle to our knowledge (they may distort our interpretation) or a source of our knowledge (they help us understand ourselves and make decisions). What we feel may be influenced by the culture we live in. However, it is believed that there may be a physiological basis to our emotions and that there are a number of universal emotions across all cultures including disgust, shock, fear and happiness. The arts have a strong connection with the emotions: we can feel moved when we read a novel or poem, look at a painting or listen to music. The arts can express emotions, and also influence our feelings. There is a significant link with ethics; feeling angry may be based on an ethical judgement that an injustice has occurred. Questions to think about might include the following.

How do our feelings relate to different areas of knowledge such as mathematics, science or human science? In what ways does our language express our feelings and attitudes? Are our emotions a reliable source of knowledge? In what ways can our feelings limit our curiosity, or motivate us to pursue certain types of knowledge?

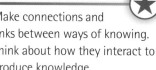

Make connections and links between ways of knowing. Think about how they interact to produce knowledge.

If you choose two ways of knowing, imagination and memory, think of how they both contribute to our knowledge. Do we imagine the past and remember the future or vice versa?

Faith

Faith is distinct from 'properly basic beliefs' such as belief in other minds or belief in the material world. There is a distinction between 'faith in' and 'faith that'. For example if by faith we mean *trust*, our faith can be based on the way we feel: faith in a particular relationship, or faith in ourselves or other people, or, for those with religious faith, faith in God. If by faith we mean a *belief* that we hold, we could have faith that particular propositions, or states of affairs, are correct, such as faith that we live in a rapidly expanding universe comprising mostly dark energy. You could consider how far your faith is shaped by the authority of people making claims about faith, or any cultural bias. You could also examine the evolutionary purpose of faith.

Faith is a significant way of knowing in religious knowledge systems, but you should also think of how it is used in other areas of knowledge. Statements of faith might include 'I have faith in God' or 'I have faith in life after death', although people might judge these very differently and look for different types of evidence to support or oppose each claim. Faith can interact with reason. In the past, studying mathematics was regarded as one of the ways to understand the mind of God. Some people view religious faith as not based on evidence. However, some religious knowledge systems may be seen as based on evidence of sacred texts or religious experiences. Knowledge claims based on faith may be regarded by some people as irrational, and by others as above and beyond the rational. For some people faith might be regarded as superior to reason on the grounds that it *doesn't* rely on evidence. Is faith a source of knowledge? How does faith connect with memory, intuition or reason? What is the difference between faith and 'blind faith'? How is faith used as a way of knowing in science, history and religious knowledge systems?

Memory

On the one hand, we might claim to know something when we remember it. On the other hand, memory is a process which we use to recall knowledge rather than the source of knowledge itself. We might assume that memory is like rewinding a DVD of our past; we recollect exactly what happens. But memory is more complicated and bound up with other ways of knowing. We use language to put memories into words, attempting to reconstruct the past, and leading to memories that have varying degrees of accuracy or even false memories. We can 'imagine' the past and use language to change our memory. Recollection may be influenced by emotion. Sense data gained through perception such as smells and tastes can lead to autobiographical memories. Hearing a song can bring back a strong sense of an event in the past.

There are many types of memory to explore, including semantic memory, episodic memory, long-term memory, short-term memory, working memory, flashbulb memory and autobiographical memory. You might explore the accuracy of eyewitness testimonies, or how far we use our memories to construct a narrative about the past. Are memories a reliable source of knowledge?

Sense perception

The sense data our brain receives is determined by the biology of our senses: sight, sound, taste, touch and smell, our sense of heat, pain, movement and balance. Other animals perceive the world very differently from us. A dog has a superior sense of smell to us, and a snake can see infrared light. Squid eyes are superior to ours; they are much better adapted to seeing in the dark. Sense data may be shaped and interpreted by other factors including our expectations, prior concepts, theories or the knowledge filter of our **paradigms**.

paradigm: a network of beliefs or a model for understanding, which can be cultural or intellectual

Our knowledge in the arts and sciences seems to depend heavily on our sense perception, and on technologies such as the microscope, which can enhance our sense perception. We cannot, however, observe ethical judgements, and we rely on other ways of knowing.

Technology exists to 'upgrade' our sense perception so that we can receive extra sensory data and communicate using thought. In March 2002 Professor Kevin Warwick (www.kevinwarwick.com/index.asp) had a surgical operation to connect a technological implant to his central nervous system. With this implant technology he is able to control an electric wheelchair and an artificial hand. Kevin Warwick became the first *cyborg*: a cybernetic organism that is part human and part machine. This application of technology raises significant ethical questions about the relationship between humans and machine intelligence. What impact do you think technology could have on our sense perception in the future?

> ★ It is important to make distinctions between sense perception that refers to knowledge gained by our senses and 'perspective' or 'viewpoint'.

> ⓘ Exploring how paradigms work is important for TOK. You might consider how far paradigms relate to what we know: they may represent reliable knowledge but if 'the map is not the territory' they may have limitations.

Intuition

Intuition is our instinct or 'gut feeling'. When we first meet someone we might have an intuitive sense about their character, about what they are like as a person. We think we know, but intuitive feelings aren't always reliable or correct. The character Elizabeth Bennett in Jane Austen's *Pride and Prejudice* has an intuition that Mr Darcy is a proud and rude man, an intuition that turns out to be wrong. We appear to have an intuition for art: we can instantly like or dislike it. Our intuition for art is shaped by other non-intuitive factors such as context, setting and expectation. In ethics some people think that we have a moral sense or an intuition about right and wrong. Mathematical intuitions might offer a flash of inspiration or a moment of insight. Andrew Wiles had a deep intuition which, combined with many years of thinking and some collaboration with other mathematicians, led to his solution in 1994 of a famous and long-standing mathematics problem, Fermat's Last Theorem. What is the justification, rationality or evidence for intuition? Does intuition have its own logic, based on 'evidence' provided by the subconscious? How far is our intuition reliable? How does it link with other ways of knowing such as emotion, language and faith?

Imagination

Imagination might be regarded as a source of knowledge. It is often associated with creativity, 'thinking outside the box' and letting our imagination take over can lead to new knowledge. In many areas of knowledge, imagination is associated with empathy, creativity, problem-solving and originality. Imagination can be used in the fourth part of the knowledge framework: you might imagine 'what if' something had been different in the historical development of an area of knowledge. A number of subjects might require you to 'imagine a scenario where *x* happens'. Imagination is needed for speculating about the past and the future. As well as being required in the arts, imagination can also be very important to mathematicians. You could consider how imagination links with memory; do we imagine the past?

> **Task: activity**
>
> Choose a way of knowing.
> 1 Describe this way of knowing using personal examples from your own experience, or your own six IB subjects, to illustrate your points.
> 2 What do you think are the strengths and weaknesses of this way of knowing as an answer to the question 'how do we know...?'

Knowledge questions

- To what extent do some ways of knowing lead to more certain knowledge than others?
- To what extent would you claim that any two areas of knowledge are different in terms of their scope, applications, key concepts and methodology?
- How far should we judge the value of an area of knowledge according to the usefulness of its applications?

Presentation task

Think about a real-life situation related to one of the following aspects of the knowledge framework: scope, applications, methodology or language and key concepts. What are some general questions that the situation raises? Give a presentation that analyses a knowledge question that arises from the situation.

Extended writing task

Write 500 words on one of the following questions:

1 Outline the contribution of key thinkers to the historical development of an area of knowledge. Find out who the key thinkers are and what their contribution to knowledge was. For example, what contributions to knowledge in the human sciences were made by either Foucault, Marx, Durkheim or Habermas? Or, what contributions to knowledge in ethics were made by either Aristotle, Mill or Kant?

2 Choose one of the following aspects of the knowledge framework: scope, applications, methodology or language and key concepts. Explore how this aspect of the framework relates to what we know in two areas of knowledge. For example you could explore methodology in human science and history, or alternatively the scope and applications of religious knowledge systems and science.

Prescribed essay titles

1 To what extent are the various areas of knowledge defined by their methodologies rather than their content? (November 2010 and May 2011)

2 Are some ways of knowing more likely than others to lead to truth? (May 2008)

3 Compare the roles played by reason and imagination in at least two Areas of Knowledge. (November 2006 and May 2007)

Further reading and sources

Plantinga, Alvin, *'Is belief in God a properly basic belief?'* in Cottingham, John G. (Editor). 2008. *Western Philosophy: An Anthology.* Blackwell Philosophy *Anthologies.*

Kahneman, Daniel. 2011. *Thinking, Fast and Slow.* Allen Lane, the Penguin Group.

Stangroom, Jeremy. 2009. *Einstein's Riddle: Riddles, Paradoxes and Conundrums to Stretch Your Mind.* Bloomsbury, USA.

5 Mathematical knowledge framework

Introduction

In many respects mathematics could be regarded as the most perfect system of knowledge we have. It is elegant, beautiful, simple, systematic, readily repeatable, and many of its theorems are supported by proofs. But the price of its perfection is that it is largely disconnected from the real world. As Einstein once put it, *'Insofar as the statements of mathematics are certain, they do not refer to reality; and insofar as they refer to reality, they are not certain.'* One of the purposes of this chapter is to explore what implications this claim has for knowledge generally and mathematical knowledge in particular.

Einstein's claim may strike you as strange. After all, as you look around you may see fifteen fellow-students in your class. You may find yourself sitting at a rectangular desk, have travelled to school in a vehicle with round wheels, and done your homework last night on a computer controlled entirely by operations in binary arithmetic and logic gates. Number, shape (geometry) and logic seem to be as rooted in the real world as anything could be. The problem is that the instances of mathematical concepts we have in the world are only ever approximations.

Numbers

Counting is a human activity that is believed to extend back well before written history began. It is an activity that we tend to take for granted and yet number theory is perhaps one of the most difficult aspects of mathematics. Some ancient peoples, and even some ethnic groups today (such as the Piraha of Brazil), only had words for *one, two* and *many.*

We now mostly count in groups of ten (what we call the decimal system) but it has not always been so. The Babylonians, for example, used the hexadecimal system based on groups of 60. The first evidence we have of a decimal system comes from Aryabhata, a Hindu mathematician born in 476 CE.

Use the knowledge framework to make comparisons and links between mathematics and other areas of knowledge. Identifying similarities and differences between different areas of knowledge is one way to show your analytical skills.

Compare the historical development of mathematics with the historical development of other areas of knowledge. Think about the following:

- How have significant developments in the field of mathematics shaped the way we do mathematics today?
- Is mathematical knowledge discovered or invented?
- How does the creation or discovery of mathematical knowledge differ from other areas of knowledge?

Real-life situation

Aly has two small bars of chocolate and Risa has one large bar. We might say that Aly has twice the number of chocolate bars as Risa, and there are three chocolate bars altogether. But if they break up all the chocolate into equal-sized squares, Risa has more pieces than Aly. Although Risa had fewer chocolate bars than Aly, she had more chocolate. To what extent does counting relate to quantity?

The way we learn about numbers shapes the way we think of them. Take, for example, the natural numbers: 1, 2, 3, . . ., which are so familiar to us. Small children learn to count by applying them to objects like bricks, balls or apples.

We may not doubt that there are three apples in the picture. If we added two more, there would be five apples, whereas if we ate two, there would be one. But what happens if we eat four? Immediately there is a problem: we cannot eat more apples than we have; the natural numbers do not extend simply in this way to negative numbers. We need a different kind of concept before we can deal with negative numbers.

Some people struggle all their lives with negative numbers and algebra because of the strong associations they have built between numbers and objects.

> Many students like to give 1 + 1 = 2 or something similar as an example of mathematical truth. This is *not* recommended. If you are going to write about mathematics in your TOK essay or presentation, you should use examples from your mathematics lessons and your own experiences.

Task: think about

- Why do we need negative numbers?
- We take zero for granted but people did without it for thousands of years. What might our world be like without it?
- How might our world be different if we only had number words for *one*, *two* and *many*?

Task: activity

Try to find out when humans first began to use zero and negative numbers. Which civilisation invented them?

If you look at any three actual apples they will not all be the same. Every apple is unique, so what we are counting are three *similar* things belonging to a particular class that is an **abstraction** from the world of apples. It is the ability to work with abstractions that gives mathematics its power in practice. And it is important in mathematics that we are able to move away from objects such as apples or chocolate bars into the world of abstractions if we are to avoid becoming confused.

> **abstraction**: a generalised concept usually derived from many specific instances

Geometry

Let us turn now to geometry and consider the circle. We all know what a circle is; we can draw one using compasses and some of us can write down the algebraic equation of a circle. We can see circles in many places in the world around us, but although the algebraic equation is precise, a drawing of a circle is only an approximation, and the wheels on the school bus are very poor approximations of circles. So we have the same problem that we have with apples: instances of circles are imperfect examples of a hypothetical perfect circle. We can think about circles, and do geometry and algebra with them, but we cannot find a perfect circle anywhere.

Euclidean geometry, in which the properties of circles are explored with great ingenuity and to exhibit great beauty, is a fiction in the sense that none of these perfect objects exists except in our minds.

> In Euclidean geometry a triangle on a plane can be shown to have the property that its angles always add up to 180° using a mathematical proof based upon Euclid's five axioms. Whether there has ever been or could ever be such a triangle outside the mind of the mathematician is an entirely different matter to which mathematics has no answer.

Task: think about

Why can't there be such things as perfect circles or straight lines in the real world?

So far, then, we have seen that the trouble with mathematics is that the things it studies and whose properties it explores with such great certainty do not actually exist. To this extent mathematics justifies the first half of Einstein's claim: *insofar as the statements of mathematics are certain, they do not refer to reality*. But what about mathematics when we apply it to the 'real world'? All around us we see examples of constructions and technologies that would not be possible without mathematics.

Applied mathematics

When engineers build bridges and other constructions they use theories and formulae that invariably take a mathematical form. To support traffic of such-and-such total mass the bridge needs to be made of girders of *this* density, *this* length, breadth and thickness connected by welds and bolts of *this* strength which will, when assembled, comfortably support traffic of *this* total mass doing *these* speeds with *these* impact characteristics as things bump up and down. Engineers try to make sure that bridges do not suffer from the kind of defects that led to the Bay Bridge disaster in 1989.

Every single piece of information in an engineer's plan involves measurements of quantity; every specification makes references to size and number; no element of the design is free from mathematical terms and quantities. How, then, does mathematics not relate to the real world?

The short answer is that, although all these characteristics of the bridge or any other engineering project use mathematical quantities and theories, they are all *approximate*, and succeed only because of the generous *tolerances* that ensure that

Compare the scope and applications of mathematics with other areas of knowledge. Think about the following:

- What kinds of practical problems can mathematics be applied to? How do these problems differ from those in other areas of knowledge?
- What are the unanswered questions in mathematics?
- To what extent does the value of mathematics lie in its applicability to problems in the 'real world'?

On 17 October 1989, an earthquake severely damaged the Bay Bridge, San Francisco, causing 68 deaths.

Compare the extent to which personal knowledge is significant in mathematics with the importance of personal knowledge in other areas of knowledge. Think about the following:

- How do individuals contribute to mathematics?
- What responsibilities does a mathematician have as a result of his or her mathematical knowledge?

whatever imperfections there may be in the theory or the manufacture of the components, there is still a huge margin for error between the theoretical maximum load on the bridge and the actual breaking-strain. This is true even in the world of computing. Although computers appear to be predictable and certain, they do not operate according to the theory of binary arithmetic as it is in mathematics. Computer circuits have a considerable amount of cross-checking built into them to prevent errors arising.

Neither mathematical numbers nor engineering and physical theories usually claim to describe the world *precisely*: they aspire to describe it as well as they can while leaving plenty of margin for error. Mathematics is an incredibly useful tool and it underpins most of the research in the natural and human sciences, but its certainty is found in the abstract, rather than in the real world.

Using applied mathematics has led to impressive constructions and innovative technologies that have changed the world we live in, but there is always a trade-off between safety, cost, precision and margins for error. We could, for example, build cars as strong as tanks; they would be much safer to drive in, but they would be so slow and expensive that few would buy them. Mathematics helps us to say what the optimum trade-offs are and what the margins of error should be, but only as a best estimate, not as an absolute certainty. So we have seen that the second half of Einstein's statement is also justified: *insofar as the statements of mathematics refer to reality, they are not certain.*

Task: think about

Calculating the time you need to get to school each morning involves applying mathematics to a real issue. You need to leave a margin for error if you want to avoid being late. Even then, an unexpected traffic jam, a delayed bus or a puncture in your bicycle tyre may still make you late if your margins are not big enough.

What other calculations do you make that require margins of error? (Think about practical work in the science laboratory or cooking dinner.)

Mathematical proof

Mathematical knowledge is thought to be certain because it is subject to rigorous forms of deductive reasoning to provide us with mathematical proofs. Only when something in mathematics is proved do we grant that it is true. Or so we say. But what is proof?

People often think that proof establishes truth: 'There! I've proved it! It must be true!' But in reality proofs do no more than *preserve* truth; they do not create it or add to it. They say, in effect, that if you grant us certain assumptions (premises, axioms), and we apply the laws of logic (deductive reasoning) correctly, the conclusions we come to – sometimes called *theorems* – will be as true as those assumptions. In other words, proof only ever tells us what we have already assumed.

Be very careful of using the word *proof* in anything but a mathematical sense. Mostly when people say they have 'proved' something, they really mean they have provided evidence for it. However, evidence does *not* constitute proof.

Task: think about

If proofs don't tell us anything new, why are they so important in mathematics?

Axiomatics

Mathematicians like to reduce the number of assumptions to as small a set as possible so that they have to assume as little as possible. These assumptions are called **axioms**. Axioms are often thought to be self-evidently true. In other words, they seem so obviously true that people don't question their truth.

Sometimes mathematicians start with a set of axioms and see what happens to the original system if they change one or more of them. It was making changes like this that led to non-Euclidean geometries in which some results of classical Greek geometry are no longer true. In spherical geometry, for example, it is not true that the angles of a triangle must add up to 180 degrees.

axiom: a starting point in reasoning that is accepted as true

A riddle

Imagine you leave your house and walk 10 km due south. You then turn 90° left and walk 20 km due east before turning 90° left again and walking 10 km due north, only to find a bear on your front doorstep. What colour is the bear?

The point of this riddle is that it neatly illustrates different axiomatic systems. If we were to sketch these instructions on a plane as we do in Euclidean geometry we would end up 20 km east of our starting point and the riddle would make no sense. But if we apply spherical geometry, when we start at the North Pole, we end up back at the same point. Knowing this is what tells us that the bear must be a polar bear, so the answer is white.

Mathematicians do not usually just make up a set of axioms and see what they can prove from them. Instead they tend to take an extended system and reduce it to axioms. Then they try to show all the original theorems can be proved from those axioms. This helps to ensure mathematical consistency within the system.

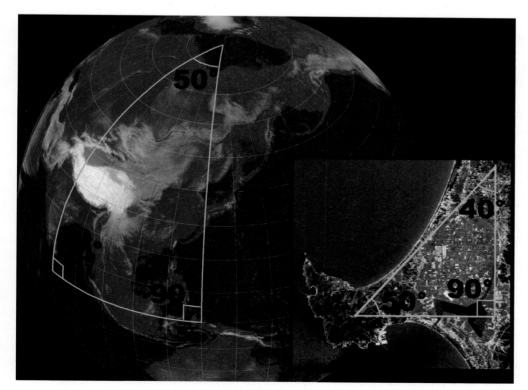

Spherical geometry of the Earth. In spherical geometry the angles of a triangle do not add up to 180°.

Different axiomatic assumptions give rise to different types of mathematics. This creates another problem for mathematical knowledge: it appears to be certain yet completely *arbitrary*. If we can pick and choose between sets of axioms, how can we say that one set of true statements proved from one set of axioms is better than an incompatible set of true statements proved from another set of axioms?

Because we have to *assume* that the axioms are true, the truth of theorems based upon them is only as good as the truth of the axioms we started with. In other words, mathematical truth is only true in the system in which it is established, and it is not necessarily a truth about the real world.

Logic

Logic is the study of valid forms of reasoning. There are different types of logic defined by different rules of inference. Deductive reasoning is one form of formal logic. Take the following example:

Premise 1	All rectangles have four sides.
Premise 2	A square is a rectangle.
Conclusion	Therefore, a square has four sides.

This is a very straightforward example and it is true *as long as both premises are true*. It offers us certainty but does not tell us anything that we do not know or assume to start with. Most school mathematics follows the rules of deductive reasoning.

Not all logic is quite so straightforward. Some logics (called modal logics) address things like *possibility* where the logical connections between 'certain', 'possible', 'likely' and so forth are built into the deductions.

A simple example might be:

Premise 1	Some quadrilaterals are trapezoids.
Premise 2	This shape is a quadrilateral.
Conclusion	Therefore, this shape could be a trapezoid.

This time, there is no certainty, only a possibility, and again we don't learn anything new. These are simple examples, but the same considerations hold true for more complex mathematical problems.

> **Task: think about**
>
> What difference will it make to our conclusions if our first premises begin with *all*, *many*, *some*, *only*, *few* or *no*?

When following the rules of deductive reasoning, it is important that we begin with the general and move to the particular and not the other way around. For example, we would be wrong to say:

> A square is a rectangle.
> A square has four sides of equal length.
> Therefore rectangles have four sides of equal length.

In the examples of deductive reasoning so far, we have been assuming our premises to be true and focusing our attention on the validity of the deductions.

Compare the methodology used to gain mathematical knowledge with methodologies used in other areas of knowledge. Think about the following:

- Many mathematicians regard imagination and intuition as important ways of knowing in mathematics. Compare their importance in mathematics with that in other areas of knowledge.

- Deductive reasoning is an essential skill in mathematics. To what extent is it necessary in other areas of knowledge?

One thing that can be very confusing in logic is that wrong use of deductions can sometimes give us the right answers. These answers are correct by coincidence, despite the poor logic.

But, even using valid logic, we are likely to draw incorrect conclusions if our premises are not true.

Although, as we have said, most school mathematics follows the rules of deductive reasoning, mathematical problem-solving involves something more. A good mathematician, when seeing a new problem, will imagine what the answer must look like before working his way to it using deduction; he must first intuit the kind of solution before providing the formal deductive proof.

Sometimes, however, logic can be counter-intuitive. We know, for example, that it is possible to make statements that we know to be true but that are not provable within a mathematical system. This was shown by *Gödel's incompleteness theorems*, which shook the mathematical world when they were first published in 1931. They show that the truth of something need not depend upon the ability to prove it.

Arbitrariness in mathematics even extends to logic in that we can choose which rules of inference to use as well as which axioms to assume. This means that a truth established by a proof using one kind of logic and one set of axioms cannot be claimed to be true in relation to a different kind of logic based upon another set of axioms, as we saw with our riddle on page 43.

> **Task: think about**
>
> If you are given the pattern: 1, 2, 3, 4, . . . and asked to give the next entry, the expected answer is probably '5'. But there are infinite *logical* possibilities that could go there. If we mark '5' as correct and other answers wrong, are we really testing people's ability to reason or are we testing their conformity to shared assumptions?

There are many things in mathematics that we believe to be true but no-one has yet been able to prove: for example, that every even number greater than 2 is the sum of two prime numbers (known as *Goldbach's conjecture*). There was once a $1,000,000 prize offered to anyone who could prove Goldbach's conjecture. Many people tried, but no-one claimed the prize. The reward expired in April 2002, but if you succeed in proving it, fame and fortune could still await you.

Mathematical imagination

Imagination is an important way of knowing in mathematics. The problems with numbers that we considered at the beginning of this chapter may be helped by imagining a number line with different numbers represented by different locations along it. We can imagine the line extending indefinitely in both directions although the line and the points along it have neither depth nor height. Although the Pythagoreans used number lines in ancient Greece, it was not until the seventh century that Brahmagupta, an Indian mathematician, wrote the first comprehensive rules for working with zero and negative numbers.

When you study *vectors* and *linear algebra* in your mathematics classes you may find it impossible to imagine six dimensions, but mathematics allows us to work with any number of dimensions. Mathematicians can solve problems in n variables by imagining them as the dimensions of an n-dimensional space, so although we may find it impossible to imagine what a six-dimensional figure might look like we can explore its properties using mathematics.

Also in your mathematics classes, you may be introduced to what are called *complex numbers*. Complex numbers are created by altering the usual rule that negative numbers do not have square roots. Examples of complex numbers are $2 + 3i$ or $4i$. What makes them complex is that they combine real numbers with an *imaginary number i* which represents $\sqrt{-1}$.

As strange as they may seem, imaginary numbers have turned out to have important applications to many real situations such as fluid dynamics, electromagnetism, quantum mechanics and fractals. Without $\sqrt{-1}$ our physics would be much poorer.

Although $\sqrt{-1}$ is undefined, and as such regarded as imaginary, it has real-life applications.

Paradoxes of infinity

One of the ways of knowing we consider in TOK is intuition, and in some situations intuition serves a very useful purpose in mathematics. For example, intuition may give us an idea of where to look for a solution to a problem, or which direction to go in as we hunt for a proof. But at other times it can mislead us. This is particularly true when we consider the mathematics of the infinite.

Most of us can understand that there are an infinite number of even numbers and an infinite number of odd numbers, and if we add them together we still have the same number of numbers, that is, an infinite number of them. We can even think of counting to infinity *theoretically*, even though we could never actually reach it: 1, 2, 3, 4, . . ., ∞. But this is only one kind of infinity.

What is far more difficult to grasp is that there are an infinite number of different infinities and some kinds of infinity are bigger than others. There are some that cannot be counted, even theoretically.

Task: activity

Watch the Ted-Ed video on 'How big is infinity' at http://ed.ted.com/lessons/how-big-is-infinity and Marcus du Sautoy's video on counting from zero to infinity, at www.guardian.co.uk/science/video/2012/apr/05/marcus-sautoy-counts-zero-infinity-video

Mathematics and reality

Numbers like π and $\sqrt{2}$ have the property that they are *irrational*: their decimal expansions go on forever without ever repeating. Therefore the number π requires an infinite number of bits of information to express it. This means that if the number π is to be real in the sense of something that could actually exist in the material world, we would need information capacity that would use up the entire mass of the universe just to write it down, and even then (since the amount of matter in the visible universe is believed to be finite), we wouldn't have finished. So if irrational numbers are not real in the sense of being things we can write down, in what sense can they be real at all?

We can manipulate $\sqrt{2}$ and π, but we can never fully know what they are.

A completely different problem arises from a difficulty with specifying the starting-conditions of mathematical systems precisely. A meteorologist called Lorenz, running a simple weather program, discovered that by entering the initial start-up data to three decimal places instead of six, the program predicted diverging and eventually completely different systems of weather.

This discovery gave rise to *complexity theory*, sometimes called *chaos theory*, which explains the sensitivity of non-linear mathematical systems to tiny variations in their starting-conditions. We now know that many systems are so sensitive that *any* change in the starting-conditions will produce divergent behaviour. Since we cannot input starting-conditions with *infinite* accuracy, we cannot project the paths of these systems with any reliability. It turns out that we cannot predict the behaviour of such systems. The best we can do is say whether the behaviour will lie within certain limits, and even that cannot be said for some systems.

In March 2013, Alexander Lee and Shigeru Kondo claimed to have calculated π to 1×10^{13} digits – a process that took them 371 days and required 44 TB of disk space. It took another 16.6 TB of disk space to store the digits in a text file.

> *For want of a nail the shoe was lost.*
> *For want of a shoe the horse was lost.*
> *For want of a horse the rider was lost.*
> *For want of a rider the battle was lost.*
> *For want of a battle the kingdom was lost.*
> *And all for the want of a horseshoe nail.*

The children's rhyme 'For want of a nail' effectively illustrates how a very small initial starting-condition (a missing nail) can have a dramatic impact on the path of a system – in this case the outcome of a battle, leading to the loss of a kingdom.

Real-life situation

When Pakistani and Indian farmers started to use the anti-inflammatory drug diclofenac to treat their cattle in 1993, the population of Indian vultures was decimated, with 97% of their population wiped out over a period of 15 years. As a result, there has been a proportionate increase in rats and feral dogs. Because rats and dogs are less efficient scavengers than vultures, there is an increased risk of diseases such as TB and anthrax, and water is being contaminated by rotting carcasses. The incidence of rabies has also risen with the increase in dogs and rats.

New drugs are tested on animals and the results are analysed mathematically to see if they are safe for use on different species of animals.

- Why might the testing and statistical analysis of diclofenac not have predicted its environmental impact?
- Why can we never know what all the effects might be?

A lone vulture where once there might have been hundreds.

Knowledge questions

- If mathematical modelling cannot make reliable predictions about complex systems, why are mathematical models regarded as so important in the human and natural sciences?
- To what extent does the analysis of statistics depend upon human interpretation?
- To what extent are we justified in believing that mathematical knowledge is certain?

Presentation task

If you want to wallpaper a room in your house, what kind of mathematics will you need to use? What information might you need and what assumptions might you need to make when calculating how many rolls of wallpaper to buy? Assuming you want to waste as little money as possible, but cannot make repeated trips to the shop if you run out of paper, how much tolerance might you want to build into your calculations?

Try to develop a knowledge question that arises from these questions.

Extended writing task

Write 500 words on one or more of the following questions:

1 What is the importance of proof in mathematics and one other area of knowledge?

2 Are mathematical concepts discovered or invented?

3 To what extent is mathematics dependent upon culture?

Prescribed essay titles

1 Mathematicians have the concept of rigorous proof, which leads to knowing something with complete certainty. Consider the extent to which complete certainty might be achievable in mathematics and at least one other area of knowledge. (November 2007 and May 2008)

2 When mathematicians, historians and scientists say they have explained something, are they using the word 'explain' in the same way? (November 2006 and May 2007)

3 Compare the roles of reason and imagination in at least two areas of knowledge. (November 2006 and May 2007)

Further reading and sources

Clawson, Calvin C. 1994. *The Mathematical Traveler. Exploring the Grand History of Numbers.* Perseus.

Einstein, Albert. 1923. *Sidelights on Relativity.* E. P. Dutton.

Hofstadter, Douglas. 1979. *Gödel, Escher, Bach. An Eternal Golden Braid.* The Harvester Press.

Puddefoot, John. 1987. *Logic and Affirmation: Perspectives in Mathematics and Theology.* Scottish Academic Press.

Stewart, Ian. 1997. *Does God Play Dice?: The New Mathematics of Chaos.* Penguin.

Stewart, Ian. 2008. *Professor Stewart's Cabinet of Mathematical Curiosities.* Profile.

6 Scientific knowledge framework

Introduction

Whereas mathematics achieves certainty at the price of detachment from physical reality, the natural sciences try to model reality in a way that is connected to it, and the connections are cross-checked through experiments. The requirement that scientific theories be *tested* in a way that is *repeatable* to produce *consistent* results regardless of who conducts the experiment gives rise to the **empirical method** of science.

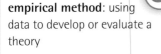

empirical method: using data to develop or evaluate a theory

As a result, scientific knowledge is often regarded as more certain than other areas of knowledge. We recognise that scientific knowledge has helped to provide us with new technologies, equipment, chemical compounds and procedures that have helped to improve our standards of living. Computers, cars and aeroplanes, plastics, medicines and surgical procedures are just a few examples of some of the innovations that have been provided through advances in our scientific knowledge. Science has also provided us with new insights into life, our planet and the universe.

People will often ask of a truth claim, 'Ahh, but is it scientifically proven?' Commercial products are frequently advertised as 'scientifically proven' to give you whiter teeth, cleaner laundry, clearer skin or glossier hair. Perhaps this is because many people view 'scientific proof' as a stamp of authenticity. But what does this really mean?

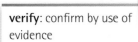

verify: confirm by use of evidence

Early scientific methods set out to **verify** scientific theories, but during the twentieth century it became clear that verification is often too ambitious. How, for example, would we verify a statement such as 'There is no planet in the universe made entirely of green cheese'? Verification by experiment would involve testing every planet and showing that it was not made of green cheese. This is theoretically possible, but practically impossible. Even though no-one seriously believes the statement to be false, it is a statement that cannot be verified.

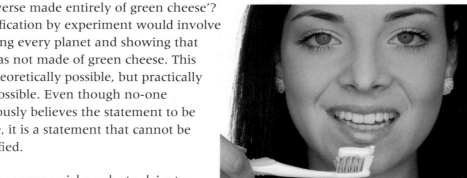

Many commercial products claim to have 'scientifically proven' benefits.

An intense debate has arisen around the issue of verification. Some people, generally referred to as **positivists**, insist that a statement that cannot be verified should be rejected from the scientific canon as meaningless. This includes all references to God, ethics and many other things of a speculative nature.

Karl Popper, in his book *The Logic of Scientific Discovery*, argued that verification expects too much of scientific methods and that we should embrace statements as scientific provided that they are **falsifiable**. By this he means that there are definite ways of being able to show that the statement is false. Using the example above, the discovery of any planet made of green cheese would falsify the theory even though we could not conduct an exhaustive search for such a planet. Therefore, according to Popper, the statement 'There is no planet in the universe made entirely of green cheese' can be regarded as scientific.

positivism: the belief that the only valid knowledge is that which is based on sensory evidence

falsifiable: able to be shown to be false; for example, 'emus are flightless birds' is a falsifiable statement because it could be shown to be false if someone were to discover a flying emu

---

Task: think about

There some scientific beliefs – for example, that the core of the sun has a temperature of approximately 15.7 million kelvin – that we do not have the technology to verify at present, but we may be able to verify in the future.

- Can we regard such statements as scientific *knowledge*?
- The statement 'God exists' is not verifiable, and is therefore meaningless to positivists. Is it falsifiable?
- Given that no-one believes there is a planet made of green cheese, what are the grounds for our confidence in such a statement?

The scientific method

There are numerous versions of the scientific method. It usually starts with a question, which may come from observation or from general research. For example, we may ask 'Why do some plants grow better than others?'

The next step is to construct a *hypothesis*. A hypothesis is a possible explanation that would answer our question. We may have noticed that chillies grow well in sunny places, so our hypothesis might be 'The more sunlight a chilli plant gets, the more chillies it will produce.'

We would then use our hypothesis to plan an experiment and predict an outcome. We might decide to grow chillies in varying positions in a garden: some in sunny spots and some in shady spots. Our prediction might be 'The plants in the sunniest parts of the garden will produce the most chillies.'

Next we would conduct the experiment, trying to control other variables as much as possible, by making sure that all our plants come from the same healthy stock, are planted in the same type of soil at the same time, and receive the same amount of water.

Once we have conducted our experiment, we will need to analyse our data to see whether or not it supports our hypothesis. If it does not, we will need to consider whether we need to modify our hypothesis and/or change our experiment.

Note that, even in the event that all of our plants growing in sunny places grew more chillies than those growing in the shade, this would not *prove* our hypothesis, it would only support it.

Compare the scope and applications of science with other areas of knowledge. Think about the following:

- The task and motivation of scientists is to understand and explain the world. How does this compare with the tasks of practitioners in other areas of knowledge?
- Are there any areas of knowledge that lie outside the scope of science?
- To what extent does the value of science lie in its applicability in the world?

The problem of data

One of the most difficult questions in science concerns the relationship between experimental data and theory. The problem is that for any set of data there will be an infinite number of theories that can explain it. No matter how many data points we have, there are an infinite number of mathematical formulae that can connect them. This means that, in addition to their experimental results, scientists have to rely upon certain assumptions about *economy* or *simplicity* when choosing hypotheses to explain their data. In other words, they will nearly always choose the simplest, or most elegant, theory. This connects deeply with belief that the universe is *intelligible* to human beings.

The principle of simplicity is one that is primarily taken on faith, although it is not always explicitly based on a religious faith as it was in the case of Sir Isaac Newton, who said *'It is the perfection of God's works that they are all done with the greatest simplicity. He is the God of order and not of confusion.'*

> Occam's razor is a scientific principle that states that, when choosing between possible hypotheses, we should choose the one that makes the fewest assumptions. This is what is meant by *economy* or *simplicity*. Scientists adopt the simplest explanations first, and will only accept a more complex explanation if it has greater explanatory power.

Of course, in the pursuit of science we have no alternative but to assume the universe is intelligible. If we argued that the universe were not intelligible, or only intelligible to beings with higher powers than humans, we could not make any progress at all.

The problem of time

Another problem for science is that our view of the universe changes with time. What were once thought to be 'final' theories of science have repeatedly been superseded.

Nobel Prize-winning physicist A.A. Michelson once wrote: *'The more important fundamental laws and facts of physical science have all been discovered, and these are now so firmly established that the possibility of their ever being supplanted in consequence of new discoveries is exceedingly remote.'* He then went on to claim that *'our future discoveries must be looked for in the sixth place of decimals'.* A few years later Einstein's special theory of relativity was published, and within another decade the entire world of physics as 'known' by Michelson had been overturned.

Task: think about

How much of what we currently believe to be true in science might be superseded or even overturned in future?

Science and reality

In education, science presents us with significant problems. We need simple ways of visualising the universe to help people come to terms with its vastness, and we also need simple ways of visualising the tiny atoms and molecules that make up the universe as we know it, so we create models. But these models are simplistic and do not show the world as it really is. This means that the models must be set aside if we are ever to understand the universe better.

The universe mapped out by Newton was a stunning intellectual achievement, and the Bohr–Rutherford model of the atom serves us very well in elementary chemistry. However, both of these models are, in a literal sense, false. The universe is not flat (Euclidean) and does not extend forever in all directions, as Newton assumed; atoms are not composed of protons and neutrons orbited by electrons in convenient shells as the Bohr–Rutherford model describes. The reality is much stranger than either of these models supposes, and much more difficult to understand.

Predictions of the way the Sun, the moon and the planets of the solar system move relative to one another are successful because the errors in the theory are extremely small, but the laws by which we calculate those orbits are technically incorrect.

You may feel a sense of déjà vu here, because we ran into similar difficulties in mathematics: *Insofar as the statements of mathematics are certain, they do not refer to reality; and insofar as they refer to reality, they are not certain.* We find that to make the universe comprehensible we have to employ theories that are not strictly true although they are sometimes a good approximation.

Compare the extent to which shared knowledge is significant in the natural sciences with the importance of shared knowledge in other areas of knowledge. Think about the following:

- How do individuals contribute to this shared knowledge?
- How does shared knowledge shape our individual perspectives?

Compare the methods used to produce knowledge in the natural sciences with those used in other areas of knowledge. Think about the following:

- How important is the use of models in science and other areas of knowledge?
- To what extent do ethics constrain the methods used to produce knowledge in the natural sciences? In what ways is this similar to or different from other areas of knowledge?

Very small positive nucleus

Negative electrons in special orbits around the nucleus

The Bohr–Rutherford model of atoms.

Task: think about

- Why is it regarded as helpful to teach physical laws and models that we know are not true?
- In the extended writing task in Chapter 1, you were asked, 'To what extent might it be more important for knowledge to be useful rather than accurate?' How might you want to revise your answer now?

Scientific theories

Two of the strongest reasons to accept scientific theories are that they *explain* known behaviour and *predict* future behaviour. A well-founded scientific theory tells us what to expect, and experiment confirms that what we expect to happen does indeed happen. For example, in chemistry, our theory about acids and bases tells us that if we add an acid to a base, we will get salt and water. And if we do an experiment to test this, the results should confirm our theory.

But it is important to realise that precision is not guaranteed. Just as we must allow tolerances in our mathematics when engineering bridges, so we must allow tolerances in physical measurements in science.

Compare the historical development of the natural sciences with the historical development of other areas of knowledge. Think about the following:

- How have significant developments in the field of science shaped the way we understand the world today?
- To what extent have different intellectual movements influenced the way we do science?

Task: activity

Look at the material on the 'Piltdown Man' at:
http://news.bbc.co.uk/1/shared/spl/hi/sci_nat/03/piltdown_man/html/#

Discovered in the early twentieth century, the skeleton had all the characteristics predicted of the 'missing link' in human evolution. But in 1953, despite having been accepted by scientists for more than 40 years, the remains were shown to be forgeries.

- To what extent do we sometimes accept evidence because we want it to confirm our theories?

Repeatability

As we have already seen, science generally insists upon repeatability as a criterion for truth. However, some of the most significant events in the world are not repeatable. It is only within a laboratory, with its controls and limitations, that repeatable conditions can be achieved, but the more controlled the environment, the less like the real world the experiment is.

Of course, in one sense, there is no such thing as a repeatable experiment: at the microscopic level, there will always be small variations, and we know from the mathematics chapter that small variations can lead to wildly different behaviour in complex systems.

By restricting the number of variables that affect the outcome of an experiment, laboratory experiments limit the applicability of their results to non-laboratory situations. We know from our experiments how things work under ideal conditions, but not how they work in reality. We seem to be back to our mathematical conundrum and close to the conclusion that, however accurate they may be, scientific theories can only model the world approximately.

Although we say that science is empirical/experimental, a great deal of its power comes from the *coherence* of the worldview it presents to us. As we have seen, experimental results that go against a popular theory are often ignored because no-one can believe that they are right. But the issue goes further than that. Any set of experimental data will usually have a lot of results that do not fit the theory: data plots may cover an area rather than fitting a line or predictable curve. Typically, we ignore the rogue results, calling them *outliers,* and we plot a smooth curve or line through the middle of the data, because we insist on the simplicity and geometry of the theory at the expense of the data.

It is widely claimed (but unsourced) that Einstein once said, *'If the facts don't fit the theory, change the facts.'* Whether or not he actually said it, there is a great deal of truth behind the saying. Scientists are often reluctant to accept data that conflicts with current theories. For example, current theories suggest that nothing can travel faster than the speed of light. When a recent Italian experiment showed evidence of neutrinos travelling faster than the speed of light, most scientists were sceptical, even though this was not the first experiment to produce such evidence. Other researchers claimed that the neutrinos were travelling at the speed of light and not faster than it. The issue of whether the data are correct or not has yet to be resolved.

Task: think about

- When you are asked to draw a 'line of best fit' in writing up a science experiment, how many of your results usually sit on that line?
- To what extent can we know what is going on in the world if we force results that do not fit our theories to conform with them?

Science and ways of knowing

Language

Language is essential for scientists to formulate their theories and publish their results; it is also central to peer review, the practice which filters and controls what is published in scientific journals. That someone's ideas and results can be written down, read, checked and evaluated by others greatly increases the ability of science to regulate itself. Often disciplines within science develop so many technical words that they seem to have a language of their own. Without knowing the technical language, it is difficult to understand the science.

Task: think about

- Why is self-regulation so important in science?
- Why can't people who are not members of the scientific community review and assess scientific theories?
- To what extent does language communicate and shape our knowledge in science?

Reason

In the chapter on mathematics, we considered deductive reasoning. The sciences also use deductive reasoning, but perhaps even more important in science is the use of **inductive reasoning**. This is when a general knowledge claim is made on the basis of repeated past experiences. Most, if not all, scientific claims are made on this basis. For example, grey whales are said to make the longest migrations of any

---

Compare the key concepts and language of science with other areas of knowledge. Think about the following:

- In science, language is highly technical to allow for greater precision. In what ways is this similar to or different from other areas of knowledge?
- Scientists use a number of key concepts including: repeatability, causation, interpretation, evidence, reliability and accuracy. How do these key concepts compare with those in other areas of knowledge?
- Some say that to be scientific, a statement needs to be falsifiable. To what extent is this true in other areas of knowledge?

inductive reasoning: when we predict future events on the basis of past experiences

A goat/sheep hybrid: an animal once thought to be impossible.

mammal, travelling up to 20,000 km per year. This is based on past observations. There is no guarantee that they will continue to migrate such long distances in future. Even scientific claims based on laboratory experiments assume that the way substances will react in the future will follow the same rules as they have in the past.

This raises the problem with inductive reasoning. No number of past experiences can prove that the pattern they record is true in all places and for all time. For example, it was long believed by scientists that animals with different numbers of chromosomes could not be crossbred and give birth to fertile offspring. This has now been shown to be false. Goats and sheep have different numbers of chromosomes and yet can be crossed to produce fertile hybrids.

Reason plays a central role in determining whether a new scientific argument or theory fits within the existing web of scientific ideas. If it does, it may be accepted; if it does not, it has to work much harder to overthrow established thinking.

In some areas of science, however, the scientific world may be prepared for fundamental changes because of problems with existing theories. When a theory is problematic, a new theory may be greeted with enthusiasm if it addresses the problems of the old theory and does not introduce too many new difficulties.

There are times when a theory may be accepted even if it seems strange to ordinary thinking and reason. Examples of this are quantum theory and general relativity. Both of these theories do not seem to follow commonly understood patterns of reason, but they have been accepted by the scientific community because of their intellectual beauty and explanatory powers.

> **Stephen Wolfram**, the man who developed Mathematica (a powerful computational program) and Wolfram|Alpha (a mathemathical search engine that is used by Siri in iPhones and iPads) believes that the universe is digital in nature and all scientific laws can be described as simple programs. He claims this will bring about 'a new kind of science'.

Task: think about

- If we have only ever observed black crows, does this mean that all crows are black?
- Space travel was once thought of as impossible. What things do we currently regard as impossible? Could they be possible in the future?

Intuition

Intuition is an important factor in the advancement of science. It helps scientists to sense where new theories and solutions to problems may be found. We saw in the mathematics chapter how important Einstein thought intuition to be, and there are many examples of scientists who have discovered a new theory by following their intuitions. For example, the German organic chemist Friedrich Kekulé claimed to have discovered the structure of benzene after dreaming about a snake biting its own tail, and intuitively connecting the dream with a ring of carbon atoms.

Like all tools, intuition can be fallible. Sometimes ideas are rejected because they seem counter-intuitive. Because intuition draws on past experiences and subconscious external cues to make a decision, it can only work when you have a relevant depth of knowledge and experience to draw on. Sometimes we may wrongly deny truths because they seem counter-intuitive, that is, they do not fit with our past experiences.

Real-life situation

In 1963, a Tanzanian schoolboy named Erasto Mpemba noticed in his cookery classes that hot ice-cream mixes froze more quickly than cold ice-cream mixes. When he asked a visiting professor why this happened, the suggestion was so counter-intuitive to his teachers and school friends that they ridiculed him. Even the professor was puzzled by the boy's observations, but was open-minded enough to run some experiments afterwards. He found that Mpemba was right, and the phenomenon became known as the Mpemba effect.

- Why is it difficult to believe that hot water freezes more quickly than cold water?
- Scientists still do not know what causes the Mpemba effect or even if it is always true. Can we call it scientific knowledge?

Sensory perception

Early scientific experiments relied on direct observation, and some of the most powerful theories ever proposed, such as Darwin's theory of evolution by natural selection, depended entirely on ordinary observations backed by detailed classification. But modern science increasingly depends on indirect observation using instruments such as electron microscopes, radio telescopes, and even particle accelerators backed by powerful computers that analyse the results of experiments statistically.

The problem with relying on such instruments is that they can introduce factors into their results that are by-products of the instruments rather than properties of whatever they are being used to study. For example, when a telescope is pointed near to the Sun, false reflections can be produced inside the optics. These can fool observers into seeing things that do not really exist.

These instruments also show us how deceptive our sensory experiences can be. Tables that feel solid are nothing of the kind when seen at atomic or sub-atomic levels; surfaces that seem flat are not flat under electron microscopy; clean plates are not clean if viewed under high magnification; things like bone, that seem fixed and permanent, are shown to be in a constant state of flux, like everything else in our bodies.

Parkes radio telescope, New South Wales, Australia, is used by astronomers worldwide to explore the universe.

Emotion

Science is often portrayed as objective and dispassionate, but scientific discoveries are made by scientists who are deeply passionate about what they do. Scientific research is often driven by personal conviction and emotional energy. Examples of this include physicist Marie Curie, who discovered radium at the cost of her own life from exposure to its radiation, and anthropologist Jane Goodall, whose passion drove her to spend 45 years studying wild chimpanzees in Tanzania.

Scientists can also become emotionally attached to their theories, and passionate advocates of theories that sometimes go against conventional wisdom and religious dogma. Passionate belief that a scientific theory is true and a strong desire to overturn conventional wisdom, despite what the majority believes, can be vital for scientific progress.

Of course, there always needs to be a balance. While some scientists may be driven by passion to make new discoveries or establish a new truth, others may be passionate in their defence of an error. Nazis rejected the theory of relativity because Einstein was a Jew, and 'creation scientists' may be driven by religious beliefs to defend their belief in a young Earth.

'Creation science' is a movement developed by fundamentalist Christians in the 1960s. It tries to find scientific evidence to counter the theory of evolution and support a theory of creation in line with the creation accounts in Genesis (the first book of the Bible). There are several different groups of creation scientists; they typically believe that the Earth is less than 10,000 years old.

Newspapers and online news broadcasts are excellent sources of TOK material in all areas of knowledge. Drawing real-life situations and examples from news stories will help you to avoid using common examples in your TOK presentation.

Real-life situation

A recent study into the effects on rats of eating genetically modified (GM) crops found that there was a significantly higher incidence of cancer in rats fed on GM crops compared with the control group. This finding led to an emotional outcry within the scientific community, with pro-GM scientists accusing the research team of having an anti-GM bias. The researchers are accused of using a breed of rats that is highly susceptible to cancer, and using biased methods in their data analysis.

- How might strong personal beliefs lead to a skewing of experimental results?
- In what ways is emotion necessary for developing new knowledge in science?
- To what extent can there be reason without emotion?

Imagination

Imagination plays a powerful role in scientific development. It allows science to reach into the microscopic world where we can speculate about quarks and gluons that nobody can sense directly, and out into the universe to other galaxies, pulsars, quasars and black holes, the properties of which challenge the very foundations of physics.

Imagination can also play its part in the more everyday world of science. While experiments are often seen as the key to science, many scientific experiments are conducted in the mind rather than in a laboratory; these are called 'thought experiments' and they have been key to many great discoveries.

The Italian physicist and astronomer Galileo Galilei conducted one of the earliest famous thought experiments by imagining tying objects with different masses together and dropping them from a great height. Simply by using his imagination and thinking it through logically, Galileo was able to show that Aristotle's theory that the speed of a falling object was dependent upon its mass was wrong.

Another famous scientific thought experiment came from Einstein. He credits his work on special relativity to a thought experiment he did as a boy, when he imagined himself chasing a beam of light through space at the speed of light.

Science fiction has often anticipated scientific advances long before they were technically possible. Nineteenth-century writers such as Jules Verne and H.G. Wells used their imagination to predict submarines and spaceships, just as Leonardo da Vinci anticipated manned flight with his designs for bird-like wings and helicopters. Imagination stimulates scientific research: once something is thinkable, others will try to make it possible.

> **Task: think about**
>
> To what extent are scientific models *imaginary*?

Compare the extent to which personal knowledge is significant in natural sciences with the importance of personal knowledge in other areas of knowledge. Think about the following:

- How do individuals contribute to our knowledge in the natural sciences?
- Would the natural sciences look different today if individuals like Galileo had acted differently?
- Would our technology be different if we had not had writers like Jules Verne?

Memory

Memory is important in science from many perspectives. As individuals we may make connections between seemingly different events by remembering similar happenings in our past, and these connections may give rise to new theories. But the most important type of memory for science is the collective memory. Having access to distributed knowledge in the written accounts of theories and experiments from around the world, and across time, allows scientists to develop and build upon the discoveries of others. This means there is no need for every individual to reinvent the wheel. If we want to create a new car, for example, we do not have to start where Henry Ford started; we can look at the cars that have been built by many others and try to improve on their designs.

Faith

We have already seen how faith in an intelligible universe, whether connected with religious beliefs or not, is essential to science. Without a deep faith in an orderly universe, it would make no sense to look for explanations of why things happen as they do based upon generalisations.

We have also seen how a scientist's personal convictions can drive him or her to pursue a theory. Einstein had such faith in his general theory of relativity that he was willing to dismiss evidence against it. The intellectual power and *coherence* of his theory was what made him believe that it had to be right.

Although he did not invent the motor car, Henry Ford (1863–1947) developed and manufactured the first affordable automobiles for a mass market, and established the Ford Motor Company.

> **Task: think about**
>
> - Where do you think Einstein's conviction might have come from? Could it have been belief in his own thinking, or belief in mathematics?
> - To what extent must you have faith in yourself if you are to successfully develop new ideas in science?

Information technology

Although not a distinct 'way of knowing' or 'area of knowledge' in the TOK framework, information technology is an increasingly important tool for knowing in all areas of knowledge, but particularly in science.

Alan Turing developed the earliest computers in Manchester in the UK. Now computers are everywhere, and microchips are present in almost every domestic appliance and motor vehicle. These developments raise several significant questions.

Task: think about

- Are there limits to what computers can achieve and, if so, what determines those limits?
- Might computers eventually develop new ways of knowing that humans will not be able to access or understand?

What practical problems can be solved with Information Technology?

Are there ethical considerations that limit the scope of technological advancement?

Real–life situation

Kismet is a robot that was designed by researchers at Massachusetts Institute of Technology (MIT) to learn social behaviours from its caretaker in ways similar to the ways a human infant learns from its mother. The work on Kismet raises interesting questions about the nature of social learning, emotion, empathy and personality.

Watch some of the videos about Kismet found at www.ai.mit.edu/projects/sociable/videos.html
- How childlike are Kismet's responses?
- Could machines ever have minds or consciousness, and how would we know if they did?

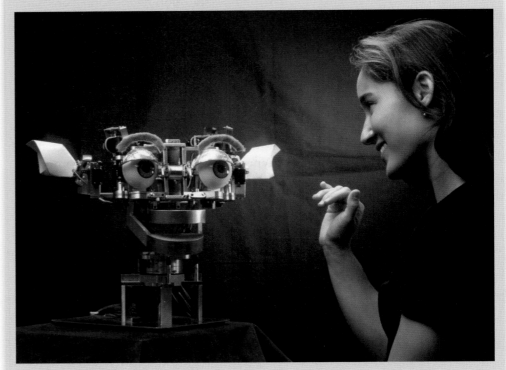

Dr Cynthia Breazeal with Kismet. Dr Breazeal developed Kismet in MIT's Artificial Intelligence Laboratory.

Knowledge questions

- To what extent must we rely on our emotions in the pursuit of scientific knowledge?
- In what ways has technology affected our ways of knowing?

Presentation task

Select one of the knowledge questions above and try to develop it. Plan a presentation based on it.

Extended writing task

Write 500 words on one or more of the following questions:

1 To what extent is our knowledge in science certain?

2 In what ways do our beliefs and cultural assumptions determine what we accept as knowledge in science and other areas of knowing?

3 To what extent must claims in any area of knowledge be falsifiable if we are to regard them as knowledge?

Prescribed essay titles

1 It is often claimed that scientific results must be replicable. Is this possible or desirable in other areas of knowledge? (November 2006 and May 2007)

2 A model is a simplified representation of some aspect of the world. In what ways may models help or hinder the search for knowledge? (November 2010 and May 2011)

3 Can a machine know? (November 2006 and May 2007)

Further reading and sources

Amos, Jonathan. *'French GM-fed rat study triggers furore'.* BBC News: Science & Environment.
　　Available at: www.bbc.co.uk/news/science-environment-19654825
Browne, Malcolm. *'The benzene ring: dream analysis'.* New York Times, 16 August 1988.
　　Available at: www.nytimes.com/1988/08/16/science/the-benzene-ring-dream-analysis.html
Brumfiel, Geoff. *'Particles break light-speed limit'.* Nature, 22 September 2011.
　　Available at: www.nature.com/news/2011/110922/full/news.2011.554.html
Davies, Paul. 2007. *The Goldilocks Enigma: Why is the Universe Just Right for Life?* Penguin.
Feynman, Richard. 1999. *The Pleasure of Finding Things Out.* Penguin.
Penrose, Roger. 1989. *The Emperor's New Mind.* Oxford University Press.
Wolfram, Stephen. 2002. *A New Kind of Science.* Wolfram Media.

7 Human sciences knowledge framework

Introduction

Human science is perhaps the broadest of the IB's areas of knowledge. It is the study of the social, cultural and biological aspects of human beings; at its most fundamental level, it addresses the question of what it is to be human.

The human sciences include most of the subjects in 'Individuals and Societies', which is Group 3 of the Diploma Programme (DP). The subjects from Group 3 that are not included in the human sciences for the purposes of TOK are history, religious knowledge systems and indigenous knowledge systems, which are considered as separate areas of knowledge.

You will see by now that the division between the various areas of knowledge and between the DP groups is somewhat arbitrary. Although, for example, psychology is listed as a human science, a great deal of psychology also falls under biological science, which is a natural science. Some of what is studied in geography can also be categorised under the natural sciences, while other aspects are strongly related to world religions and indigenous knowledge. In a similar way, language can be considered an area of knowledge as well as a way of knowing, and mathematics can be considered a language. It is important to understand that there are no clear or sharp divisions between different areas of knowledge; all disciplines interact with each other and are interdependent. The human sciences in particular overlap considerably with all other areas of knowledge in terms of the questions they investigate, the knowledge claims they make, the methods that they use to develop their knowledge, and the ways of knowing that they depend on. We can use the knowledge framework to help analyse these overlaps.

Use the knowledge framework to make comparisons and links between the human sciences and other areas of knowledge. Identifying similarities and differences between different areas of knowledge is one way to show your analytical skills.

Methodology in the human sciences

Generally speaking, a significant difference between the human and natural sciences is that the natural sciences often follow the scientific method, and experiments in natural sciences are usually repeatable by other scientists in tightly controlled laboratory studies. This is rarely true in the human sciences where new knowledge often relies on isolated case studies, non-repeatable studies, or studies that have far too many variables to control properly.

Scientists and philosophers of science have many different opinions on what constitutes a scientific method, but there is general agreement that for human sciences to be regarded as *sciences*, the methodologies used to study them must meet certain standards in terms of a *systematic* approach.

In practice, the study of individual or group behaviours is often done by conducting studies of large numbers of individuals or groups, and analysing the behaviours statistically to try to determine trends that will allow researchers to make predictions based on probabilities. For example, after analysing the behaviour of different investors in multiple situations, economists might predict a rise in stock prices following growth in the gross domestic product (GDP). This prediction will be based on investor behaviour in similar circumstances in the past. Political analysts make predictions about electoral results based on extensive polling of the population. Many times their predictions are realised, but sometimes they are not.

Task: think about

- Why must we be cautious about predicting investor behaviour for the current year based on investor behaviour in any other years, even if the financial circumstances seem similar?
- Why can circumstances only be *similar* and not *the same*? Think about all the changes that happen in the world. How might these affect investor behaviour?

Large-scale observations are not the only way of gathering data for human sciences. Other methods include case studies, observations of knowing participants, non-participatory observations, controlled experiments, surveys, statistical analysis and thought experiments. We will examine each of these and consider the roles of some of the different ways of knowing in each of them.

Case studies

A case study is a research method that is popular in various human sciences. Case studies involve detailed analysis of single individuals, groups or events, usually over a long period of time. Case studies may look at subjects as diverse as the management structure in a particular organisation, an innovative therapy in a particular care home, or the life of an individual person. They rely heavily on sense perception and language: observing details in the life of the individual or collective being studied, asking questions then interpreting and analysing responses.

Researchers also rely on reason as they try to make sense of any correlations they observe. Emotion can play a part, particularly in long-term studies. In some cases the researcher might develop an attachment to the subject, for example, a medical practitioner or psychiatrist writing up the case study of a long-term patient. In other cases the researcher may have a vested interest in interpreting results and reporting a case in a way that is consistent with his or her preferred theories. This may not be a deliberate bias; it may be a tendency of the researcher to select, reject or interpret data because he or she may think in a certain way.

Subjects for case studies are rarely typical. They tend to be selected on the basis that they offer an interesting and unusual perspective on a particular area of research. For example, a researcher into marketing strategies might conduct a case study on a company that has had a remarkably successful marketing campaign in order to try to discover which factors led to the success of that campaign.

Compare the scope and applications of the human sciences with other areas of knowledge. Think about the following:

- The task and motivation of the human scientist is to understand human beings, and their social, cultural and economic environments. How does this compare with the tasks of practitioners in other areas of knowledge?
- In the human sciences, the process of making observations alters the practices being observed. How does this compare with the effects of observation in other areas of knowledge?
- To what extent is knowledge generated by the human sciences applicable over time and place?

truisms: self-defining truths, statements which are true by definition; for example, 'we have strong feelings when we experience emotions'

Task: think about

- 'We see what we know' is a popular **truism**. How might it be more true in the human sciences than in other areas of knowledge?
- Why might it make more sense for a marketing researcher to study one very successful campaign than to compare several campaigns by different companies, selected randomly?
- To what extent can we eliminate our cultural biases and ideological beliefs when doing research into the human sciences? Should we even try to?
- What are the dangers when experts studying rare cases have particular, preferred theories? To what extent can we guard against such dangers?

ethical considerations: taking into account the set of ethical rules which govern how experiments can be conducted. For experiments on human subjects these rules include informed consent, confidentiality, and not causing harm.

Ethical considerations limit the kinds of experiment that can be conducted on human beings: for example, we cannot remove or damage parts of human brains to see what effects it causes. Sometimes, case studies can provide information that cannot ethically be obtained through experiment. For example, we can study people whose brains have been injured through accident or essential surgical procedures. Such case studies have provided neuroscientists, psychologists and philosophers with invaluable insights into the workings of the brain.

Real–life situation

In 1953 a man had a large portion of his brain surgically removed in an attempt to cure him of severe epilepsy. The surgery cured his epilepsy but left him unable to create new memories. He was able to remember events that occurred before his surgery but could not recall anything that happened after the surgery. He could only remember new pieces of information for approximately 20 seconds. Despite this, he was able to learn and remember new skills. As a result of studying this man, neuroscientists and psychologists learnt a great deal about which parts of the brain are involved in long-term and short-term memories, and how different types of memory are processed and stored in different areas of the brain.

- Although many people have epilepsy, why is this case study not repeatable?
- What are the advantages of being able to study such a rare case?
- How much can we rely on knowledge that is drawn from a sample of one?
- How might the personal involvement of doctors in cases like this affect the ways in which the cases are described?

Participatory observations

Psychology, business management, anthropology, geography and other disciplines may all, in different circumstances, use studies in which the individuals or groups they are studying *know* they are being studied: these are **participatory observations**. There are many different types and they vary in the degree to which the observers interact with those being observed. For example, an anthropologist may spend months or even years living with a remote ethnic group to study their customs and culture, and to try to get an 'inside perspective' of everyday life for that group. In other instances, a psychologist, sociologist or educationalist may run a series of 30-minute focus groups to study people's responses in an interactive environment, or to gain access to the thoughts and opinions of different social and cultural groups.

Clinical drug trials are another type of participatory observation. Often these are run as *double blind* trials. This means that neither the people taking the drugs nor

participatory observations: when researchers interact with the persons they are observing

the researchers giving the drugs know which people are in the treatment group and which are in the control group. The idea behind this is that it eliminates both the **placebo effect** in patients and any subconscious bias on the part of the researchers in the way that they treat the patients or the way in which they interpret results.

placebo effect: when patients show an improvement in their condition because they think they have been given an effective form of treatment; for example, they may feel better after being given a medication that has no active ingredient

Task: think about

- To what extent can an external observer gain an 'inside perspective' of any community or cultural group? How might language differences affect such studies?
- What differences are there between testing chemical reactions in a laboratory and testing chemical reactions inside human (or animal) bodies?

In some cases an observer may simply watch and record behaviours. Some people regard these as non-participatory observations because the observer does not directly interact with those being watched, but the knowledge of being observed is itself an interaction that has noticeable effects on the behaviour of those being observed.

Real-life situation

A long-term research project by Harvard Business School in 1927–32 sought to find what physical and psychological factors in the working environment of the Hawthorne plant of the Western Electric Company helped to increase worker productivity. It was eventually discovered that, whatever factors were adjusted (e.g. heating, lighting, working hours) and whether they were increased or decreased, productivity increased. This became known as the Hawthorne effect: productivity increases as a result of the workforce receiving greater attention.

- Do you work harder when you know your teacher is watching you?
- Do you make more of an effort when you know your work will be assessed?
- To what extent do you think the Hawthorne effect might account for athletes breaking records during the Olympic Games?
- What are the similarities between the Hawthorne effect and the placebo effect?

When a school inspection team visits your school, the inspectors make observations about the facilities of the school, the standards of teaching and learning, and the effectiveness of the management structure in your school at that time. These observations are compared with and added to observations made in other schools, and help to give governments a sense of the standards of educational provision around the country.

Do you eat differently when you have guests?

Task: think about

- To what extent do members of your family behave differently when you have visitors?
- How different are your conversations with your friends when you're alone with them compared with when there is a parent or teacher in the room?
- To what extent can we learn about the behaviour of people by observing them when they know they are being observed?

Non-participatory observations

non-participatory observations: when those being observed are unaware that they are being observed

If you ever listen in to a conversation when the people who are talking do not realise you are listening, you are being a non-participatory observer. Psychologists often use **non-participatory observations** to study the behaviour of children and animals. They can be watched through one-way windows or hidden cameras in a variety of situations.

It is more difficult to make non-participatory studies of adults because of ethical considerations. Whereas parents may give consent for their children to be studied, and animals are not afforded rights under our laws, adults must usually consent to being studied. By giving their consent, adults become knowing participants. One way psychologists try to get around this problem is to invite people to volunteer for psychological tests, and then test those who have consented in ways they are not expecting.

Be careful not to become confused by terminology when doing research, particularly in the human sciences. Not all people use the same definitions. For example, some people will describe non-interactive observations (such as school inspections) as non-participatory even though the subjects know they are being observed. When comparing types of research, you need to be clear how you are using the different terms and use them consistently.

Sometimes non-participatory observations may be made in a *covert* manner. This means people do not know they are being observed. In most cases it would be unethical for a researcher to do this, but in some circumstances it is regarded as acceptable for people such as undercover police officers or undercover agents. These covert observations are interactive in that the undercover agent must effectively join the group he or she is observing and be accepted as one of them, for example when a police officer pretends to be a drug dealer to infiltrate a drug-smuggling organisation. Only then can observations be made without the group realising it is being observed.

Task: think about

- If an undercover police officer lives and works with a drugs gang to learn more about the gang's customs, and an anthropologist lives and works with a particular ethnic group to learn more about the group's customs, how are their roles as researchers different?
- Why might we say the study by the anthropologist is participatory and the study by the undercover police officer is not?
- Which of the two observers might learn more reliable information, and why?

Controlled experiments

Controlled experiments are largely perceived as being the domain of the natural sciences, but, as we saw in Chapter 6, not all natural science is based on controlled experiments. Similarly, not all controlled experiments are done in the field of natural sciences. Experiments are a widely accepted research method in psychology, sociology, economics and other branches of human science.

The simplest models of human experimentation divide subjects into two groups: a control group and a treatment group. Subjects in both groups are treated alike except for the stimulus or condition being tested for. For example, if we were to run an experiment to test whether vitamin C supplements help to prevent colds, we would have two similar groups of people with the same gender/age/racial/socioeconomic mix. One group (the treatment group) would be given vitamin C supplements, and the other group (the control group) would be given a placebo. People participating in the experiment would not know which group they were in. As with such studies in the natural sciences, no controlled experiment can eliminate all variables, and results must be statistically analysed. A significant difference between running human experiments and natural science experiments is the ethical dimension. Human experiments are subject to much more stringent regulations than other types of experiments. These regulations include: human subjects must give informed consent, their privacy must be respected, and they must be allowed to withdraw at any time. In addition, the experiment should demonstrably involve greater potential benefits than risks.

The **Nuremberg Code** was developed in response to atrocious human experiments during the Second World War. It provides guidelines to help protect human experimental subjects from injury, disability or death.

The **Declaration of Helsinki** is a statement of ethical principles for medical research involving human subjects developed by the World Medical Association.

Real-life situation

Many new drugs are tested on subjects in less economically developed countries (LEDCs); the informed consent they sign is often in a language they do not understand. This raises serious ethical questions about exploitation. Often these subjects bear all the risks of experimentation, yet if the drug eventually comes to market, they cannot afford to use it. Of course, if drugs are not tested, we cannot know if they are safe to use.

- Why do you think many drug trials are carried out in LEDCs?
- Would paying people to take part in potentially dangerous experiments make the studies more ethical or less ethical?
- Should new drugs be tested on healthy volunteers knowing that these might cause harmful side-effects? Or should they be tested on people who are going to die anyway? What effects might a subject's overall health have on the efficacy of the drug being tested?
- Who are the main beneficiaries of drug studies: those the drugs are tested on or others?

The US Supreme Court allowed a civil lawsuit against pharmaceutical giant Pfizer for allegedly carrying out non-consensual drug tests on Nigerian children in which some children died.

Surveys

Surveys are a popular method of research in the human sciences. Surveys obtain responses from a sample of individuals in a population, from which they try to make statistical inferences about the whole population.

There are many different types of survey: some ask open questions which respondents can answer in any way they wish; others ask closed questions which may be answered with one of a few choices (usually two to five options). Surveys can also be done over the phone, by mail, in person, online, and so on. Each of these methods has several advantages and disadvantages. There is usually a trade-off between the complexity of the survey, ease of administration, the numbers of completed surveys, costs and the reliability of the results. Many of the survey methods skew the results simply by their collection method. For example, if a company puts an online survey on its website, the people who respond will be the type of people who enjoy filling in surveys and who were on the website in the first place. However many responses the company eventually gets, they will be from a particular section of the community.

A good survey is not easy to devise. People's opinions can be swayed by the ways in which questions are asked, and even by the order in which they are asked. Consider the differences in language in the following:

Students should be severely punished for handing in late work.	*Yes / No*
There should be consequences for students who hand in late work.	*Yes / No*
Students should get off scot-free for handing in late work.	*Yes / No*

It is easy to see how the way in which a statement is worded might influence the responses received. Which words used in each of the sentences above most influence your choice of answers?

- If survey results are easily skewed and people's opinions are easily swayed, how much credibility can we give to surveys?
- Many countries prohibit electoral polls in the days just before the election because the results of electoral polls can cause voters to change their votes. What might that tell us about how people vote?
- Can you think of some of the advantages and disadvantages of some of the different survey methods you have encountered?

Statistical analysis

Although statistical analysis is listed as a methodology for the human sciences, it is not an independent method; statistical analysis requires data and the data are provided by other methods such as those outlined above.

Statistical analysis is very useful, but it is only as good as the data it is applied to. If irrelevant factors are observed, or relevant factors observed badly, or if poor questions are asked, or good questions are classified poorly, the conclusions of any analysis will be unreliable.

Also, statistical analyses always require interpretation, and interpretation is always based on assumptions. As we saw in the chapter on mathematics, however accurate the reasoning process, the conclusions we draw are only as good as the assumptions on which our reasoning is based.

Task: think about

- It is often said that statistics can be used to support anything. To what extent do you agree?
- Many online news reports include a poll asking readers for their opinions. How well do you think these polls reflect public opinion and why?
- When filling out a survey we sometimes find ourselves ticking answers we don't really agree with because there is nothing closer to the answer we want to give. How much do you think we can rely on data generated by such surveys?

Thought experiments

Thought experiments are perhaps most commonly associated with philosophy and physics, but also have a place in law, ethics, psychology, economics, cognitive science, business studies, political science and other fields within the human sciences. As we saw in Chapter 6, a thought experiment uses an imaginary situation to try to understand a real issue. By applying reason to an imaginary situation, the philosopher or scientist can challenge current theories and further understanding. One famous example from philosophy is the 'Ship of Theseus'. The experiment describes a wooden ship that has been preserved for hundreds of years, thanks to regular repairs and maintenance. As old planks rot they are replaced with new ones, until a time comes when not one part of the ship is an original fitting. The question is, is this still the Ship of Theseus? If it is not, when did it stop being the same ship?

Compare the key concepts and language of the human sciences with other areas of knowledge. Think about the following:

- In the human sciences, language has been the dominant medium by which practitioners have passed on their knowledge. In what ways is this similar to or different from knowledge transmission in other areas of knowledge?
- A human scientist uses a number of key concepts including: correlation, interpretation, evidence, bias, statistical significance and reliability. How do these key concepts compare with those in other areas of knowledge?

The Ship of Theseus. How much of the original ship can be changed before it ceases to be the same ship?

How do thought experiments generate new knowledge in the human sciences and other areas of knowledge?

Many philosophers have developed the 'Ship of Theseus' thought experiment and there are several modern equivalents exploring the concept of identity.

Task: think about

- The identity problem comes up in many situations. In what areas of knowledge might it be most important?
- What are the advantages and disadvantages of thought experiments compared with practical experiments?

Real–life situation

Migration is an issue that affects every country in one way or another. Some countries have large numbers of immigrants moving there; others have large numbers of people emigrating. Some countries have large numbers of people moving around within the country. Even countries with relatively stable populations find that tourism and/or agricultural work can create seasonal migrations.

There are several different types of migration, and many different reasons for each of them. All of the methods outlined in this chapter have been employed in some ways to study human migration.

- What would be the advantages and disadvantages of each of these methodologies (case studies, participatory observations, non-participatory observations, controlled experiments, surveys, statistical analysis and thought experiments) if you wanted to learn more about human migratory patterns?
- What would be the advantages and disadvantages of each of these methodologies if you wanted to understand the motives behind human migration?
- If you wanted to explore the issues related to refugees, what methods of investigation might you employ and why?
- How might our personal assumptions, past experiences and personal preferences affect our choices of methodology?

Knowledge questions

- Do we rely more on reason or emotion when determining what research methodologies we will use in the human sciences?
- To what extent is our knowledge shaped by the methodologies we choose to explore a subject area?

Presentation task

Select one of the knowledge questions above. How might you develop it for a presentation? What other real-life situations might your knowledge question apply to?

Extended writing task

Write 500 words on one or both of the following questions:

1 To what extent are the 'human sciences' really *science*?

2 To what extent can we make observations without affecting what we observe?

Prescribed essay titles

1 Examine the ways empirical evidence should be used to make progress in different areas of knowledge. (November 2009 and May 2010)

2 Discuss the strengths and limitations of quantitative and qualitative data in supporting knowledge claims in the natural sciences and at least one other area of knowledge. (November 2009 and May 2010)

3 'We see and understand things not as they are, but as we are.' Discuss this claim in relation to at least two ways of knowing. (November 2009 and May 2010)

Further reading and sources

Attenborough, David. 1996. *Human Planet*. DVD. BBC.

Baggini, Julian. 2011. *The Ego Trick*. Granta.

Hall, Johansson and Strandberg. 2012. *'Lifting the veil of morality: choice blindness and attitude reversals on a self-transforming survey'*. PLoS ONE 7(9): e45457.

Available at: www.plosone.org/article/info%3Adoi%2F10.1371%2Fjournal.pone.0045457

8 History knowledge framework

Introduction

In this chapter we examine the knowledge claims made in history. Our historical knowledge is arguably one of the most important bodies of shared knowledge, and our mechanism for passing on knowledge to future generations is one of our successes as a species. History studies the recorded past using a method based on the concepts of evidence, reliability and accuracy. We have an appetite for the past, shown by the popularity of historical novels, blockbuster films with historical themes, historical TV documentaries and the numbers of people who flock to museums, historical monuments and galleries. Furthermore, our personal knowledge of the modern world depends on a good knowledge and understanding of our shared historical past. The identity of a country is shaped by its collective memory of its military, political and socioeconomic history. In this chapter we explore how, in our search for historical knowledge, we make use of the different ways of knowing available to us, including language, memory, reason and imagination.

Rosalie and Geoff are discussing historical knowledge.

Rosalie: Historians tell a tale of the past that's no different from a novel. History is fiction. It's made up.

Geoff: How can that possibly be true for all historians?

Rosalie: There's no such thing as the past. There's only the present, and historians' narratives tell us stories that appeal to our modern imagination and interest today.

Geoff: Perhaps you need to use your imagination? Governments around the world keep national archives which contain millions of documents covering hundreds of years of history in many different countries. We can use these to find out what is significant and find out what there is to know about the past. History is 'out there' waiting to be discovered.

Use the knowledge framework to make comparisons and links between history and other areas of knowledge. Identifying similarities and differences between different areas of knowledge is one way to show your skills of analysis.

Compare the scope and applications of history with other areas of knowledge. Think about the following:

- The task and motivation of the historian is to know about the past. How does this compare with other areas of knowledge?
- The historian needs to conform to standards and conventions such as intellectual honesty, accuracy and sound judgement and interpretation of the evidence. How does this compare with standards and ethical limits in other areas of knowledge?

Historical knowledge

History is more than just assembling the facts of past events; it is an attempt to understand in a critical way the causes, course and consequences of those events. One way to understand different ways of doing this is to look at historiography – how historians describe what they do, and the various ways in which they do it. A good starting point is to consider the knowledge question 'Can we be sure if our construction of historical knowledge is based on an accurate, **objective** view of the past or our own **subjective** interpretation?' Simply put, is history something we discover or do we invent it?

On the one hand there appear to be indisputable and objective historical facts 'out there' that form part of our shared historical knowledge. We know that the leader of the Indian independence movement, M.K. Gandhi, was shot on 30 January 1948. This is a historical fact that can be checked against sources. We are making a very different type of claim by asserting that 'The life and work of M.K. Gandhi paved the way for a modern Indian democracy and, without him, Nehru (1889–1964) would never have become India's first prime minister in 1947.' That claim is based on an interpretation of the evidence that weaves a meaningful narrative. Historical judgements like these might be less certain than basic facts because they are interpretations.

One reason why history is important is because it can help us remember and give us a sense of national or global identity. The historian can focus on Asian, Middle Eastern, West Indian, European, Australasian or Latin American history. However, there are ethical considerations that limit the scope of the enquiry. It would be unethical to make claims that are not based on a sound and reasonable analysis of the evidence. The following example illustrates why. It is part of our shared knowledge that between 1939 and 1945 around 5.5–6 million Jews were killed in Europe, an act of genocide known to Jews as the Shoah but often referred to as the Holocaust. In the UK courts in 2000 David Irving sued the American historian Deborah Lipstadt and her publishers, Penguin Books, for libel. Lipstadt had claimed in her book *Denying the Holocaust: The Growing Assault on Truth and Memory* (1993) that Irving had deliberately misinterpreted the evidence and was a Holocaust denier.

objective view of history: the idea that there is a truth or reality that is independent of my own personal perspective; for example, the claim that 'there are objective truths about the past'

subjective view of history: the idea that truth and reality depend upon my own personal perspective; for example, the claim that 'what I know about the past is based on my own thoughts, feelings, imagination and interpretation'

The leader of the Indian independence movement, M.K. Gandhi (1869–1948). To what extent are historical facts more certain than historical interpretations?

Irving took the case to court in an attempt to clear his name. The case involved the court examining the evidence, which included his personal interpretation of the Holocaust, but also evidence from others who did not share his extreme minority view. Irving claimed that historians can interpret evidence as they see fit and are usually exempt from the rigours of a courtroom challenge and the need to prove their case. In this case Richard Evans, a historian from the University of Cambridge, was the expert witness. He showed that Irving had deliberately distorted the evidence, and Irving lost his case.

This shows that a historical interpretation is not necessarily justified when tested against the standard of the law. But history is seldom tested against this standard, and most historians would accept that their work should conform to certain commonly accepted standards and conventions, such as honesty, diligence and accuracy. Even before the court case, Irving was believed to have stepped outside of these boundaries, in the opinion of his many critics. To deny the Holocaust is a highly offensive claim to make and is illegal in some European countries.

Here are some examples of unresolved or unanswered historical questions:
- Is history a human science?
- Is eyewitness testimony a reliable source of evidence?
- How do we make sense of vast numbers of sources?
- How much is enough source material and information to gather before we can claim knowledge and understanding of an event?

Task: think about

- What is the study of history about and why do you think it is important?
- What are the ethical factors that might influence the task of the historian?

Methods used to produce historical knowledge

All history must be based on a sound interpretation of the evidence. Historians use an empirical method based on interpretation of historical sources. A historian has many tools at his or her disposal. Here we will consider four of them: language, reason, imagination and memory.

Language

Throughout history there have been many recorders of history: the 'Father of History', Herodotus, who lived in ancient Greece in the fifth century BCE, was one of the earliest. History can be described as the study of the recorded past, with written records and written documents forming the basis of much of the evidence. Historians also use non-written sources such as artefacts and archaeological finds.

The social history of the American West focuses on the ordinary lives of the settlers and the Native American Indians. To gain knowledge of this period from the nineteenth century, historians might select different types of **primary sources**: Native American artefacts such as headdresses and beadwork will be interpreted differently from a written primary source from the time, such as the diary written by Laura Ingalls Wilder, who was a settler. Historians will interpret the sources and check their reliability and accuracy.

When you write about history in TOK, Think about the following:

- What knowledge claims are made by historians?
- How certain are their knowledge claims?
- What counter-claims are made by other historians?
- What is your own critical analysis of the knowledge claims?

Compare the key concepts and language of history with other areas of knowledge. Think about the following:

- In history, language has been the dominant medium by which historians have passed on their knowledge. In what ways is this similar or different in other areas of knowledge?
- A historian uses a number of key concepts, including continuity, change, causation, interpretation, evidence, reliability and accuracy. How do these key concepts compare with other areas of knowledge?

---

primary source: a document or physical artefact that was created during the time of study

Reason

Our classification of sources as primary or secondary involves a judgement based on reason. A primary source might be an artefact or a written document from the time being studied. A historian's interpretation of a primary source can produce a **secondary source**, which is a source that presents information found elsewhere. A secondary source, written after the event, often includes historical interpretation and may comment on primary materials.

Historians use reason to evaluate sources and also use reasoning as part of their method. Identifying particular pieces of evidence, say archaeological finds, to form general conclusions about life in a specific era is an example of inductive reasoning that historians use routinely.

> **secondary source**: a document or physical artefact that was created much later than the time to which it relates or by someone not directly involved

Real-life situation

The Qin Shihuang UNESCO World Heritage site in Shaanxi province in western China is one of the world's richest archaeological reserves. The extraordinary terracotta warriors, horses and artefacts excavated there are primary sources used by historians to gain knowledge of Chinese emperors. For example, historians have analysed the statue army in the mausoleum and have reasoned that it represents the exact number of guards in the imperial army at that time.

Historians also use deductive reasoning. They may have a general hypothesis and look for particular evidence to support it. One general hypothesis is that great people are the agents of change in history. The historian A.J.P. Taylor (1906–90) identified Napoleon, Bismarck and Lenin as examples of great individuals who have changed the course of history. Taylor looked for evidence to show how these individuals changed the world.

On the other hand, the revolutionary communist philosopher Karl Marx (1818–83) proposed that economic and technological factors are the causes of change. Marx looked for evidence for the overarching theory that conflict between the social classes created a pattern of events that developed independently of the actions of individuals.

> When you write about history in TOK, explicitly identify any errors in reasoning or assumptions made in knowledge claims or arguments.

To what extent do you think that change is caused by economic and technological factors or the actions of individuals?

You could readily spot evidence that might fit this hypothesis today: the global economic recession or digital technology might be identified as factors that determine change rather than the actions of individuals.

Our view of the past depends on our rationality. The view that change is caused by *both* long-term social and economic trends *and* the actions of individuals is based on a rational judgement about the relative importance of different causes of events. Reason enables us to make sense of the past, interpret evidence and identify patterns in history.

Imagination

Imagination might seem to be the enemy of the historian. Whereas a historical novelist can embellish the facts and be free to innovate beyond the evidence, historians are usually limited by their own conventions. In his book *Imperium,* (2006), the novelist Robert Harris writes literary fiction about the famous Roman orator and lawyer Cicero (106–43 BCE) and is not constrained by the same need to base his narrative on the evidence.

The historian has a responsibility to stay true to the evidence. R.G. Collingwood (1889–1943) commented that 'As works of imagination, the historian's work and the novelist's do not differ. Where they do differ is that the historian's picture is meant to be true.' On the other hand, some historians have used imagination as a tool for making the past more real and more immediate to modern readers. In *The Black Death: A Personal History* (2008), the historian John Hatcher combines history with fiction. He reconstructs the experience of ordinary people living in a Suffolk village during the time of the Black Death in mid-fourteenth-century Britain, using a combination of archival evidence and his own imagination. Constructing history from the distant past, where source material and artefacts are limited, requires an empathetic and imaginative leap. To make the medieval period more accessible to his modern readership, he combines hard historical data with fictional conversations with people from the time.

Memory

People who were present at an event and experienced it first hand as eyewitnesses can give very important testimonies based on their direct memory, which can be very powerful. The Italian–Jewish writer Primo Levi's book *If This Is a Man* (1947) offers a first-hand account of the inhumanity that he experienced having survived in Auschwitz from February 1944 until the camp was liberated on 27 January 1945.

On the other hand, eyewitness testimony is not always a reliable source of information that can be taken at face value. People's memories may be inaccurate or unreliable. Memory can be affected by **hindsight bias**.

Like all sources, memoirs and personal memories of eyewitnesses need to be interpreted. While they may appeal to our emotions and communicate the reality of an event very effectively, the historian needs to use their own judgement and consider them carefully. For example, a memoir by Albert Speer, Hitler's Armaments Minister 1942–5, has been challenged because it does not fit with other evidence. In his book *Inside the Third Reich* (1970) Speer gives his personal account based on his own memories but glosses over his use of concentration camp slave-labour and thus his own involvement in the Holocaust.

hindsight bias: the tendency to imagine that events in the past were more predictable than they actually were. It's the thinking that goes along the lines 'I should have known that . . .'

Areas of knowledge and ways of knowing are connected. Think about how historians use different ways of knowing to gain knowledge. Ways of knowing are not separate and isolated from each other, and different ways of knowing can interact: for example, a historian might use their reason and imagination to understand the past.

Compare the methodology used to gain knowledge in history with other areas of knowledge. Think about the following:

- A historical fact is that the USA invaded Mexico in 1846. An explanation of the war would require interpretation of the evidence. How might historical facts and explanations compare with other areas of knowledge?
- Historians use a method based on the concepts of evidence, reliability and accuracy, analysis, imagination and reason. How does this compare with other areas of knowledge?

Task: think about

- In what ways do historians use reason as a tool in their search for historical knowledge?
- In what ways might it be appropriate or inappropriate for a historian to use their imagination in their search for historical knowledge?
- What part does language play in our search for historical knowledge?
- How might the assumptions behind the historical method compare with the assumptions behind methods in other areas of knowledge?

Task: activity

Research into and define some of the following concepts which historians might make use of: hypothesis, narrative, interpolation, significance, selection, reliability, accuracy, perspective, paradigm, speculation, counter-factual thinking, explanation and motivation. Discuss the relevance of these concepts to the historian.

Shared knowledge

Knowledge of minds

If we claim to know something about the past we might investigate reports of what actually happened. For example, the assassination of the US President John F. Kennedy in Texas on 22 November 1963 was investigated by the Warren Commission, which produced an 888-page report and concluded that there was one assassin, Lee Harvey Oswald. The Warren Commission provided detailed records of what happened but the findings have since been questioned. It would be very difficult to know what happened from the 'inside', from the perspective of Lee Harvey Oswald, as this famous case never came to trial because Oswald was shot by Jack Ruby.

The historian R.G. Collingwood claimed that the task of the historian is to understand both the 'outside' of a historical event as well as the 'inside' of the event. Collingwood makes the distinction between our knowledge of the outside of an action, in this case the shots fired, and the inside of an action, the thoughts of the assassin that motivated the action.

Task: think about

If the study of history is concerned with understanding the thoughts, motives and mind-set of people from the past, how is it similar to or different from the study of psychology?

Knowledge of patterns

Our historical knowledge and understanding might affect how we judge political situations today. For example, our interpretation of the Bulgarian Crisis, also known as the Balkan Crisis, of the mid-1870s might have an impact on how we judge a country's modern foreign policy. The Bulgarians had been ruled by Turkey since the fourteenth century. In 1876 the Bulgarians revolted against Turkish rule and in response the Turks were reported to have killed between 10,000 and 25,000 Bulgarian men, women and children. The political response to this in the UK was mixed. On the one hand, the British Prime Minister Benjamin Disraeli (1804–81) was reluctant to believe the reports and intervene on behalf of the Bulgarian people. On the other hand the leader of the Liberal Party, William Gladstone (1809–98), was morally outraged by the atrocity and supported intervention.

Today the moral and political question remains: when and under what circumstances should the United Nations sanction military intervention by foreign countries? Our shared historical knowledge of foreign intervention might shape our understanding of what is an appropriate response. We might consider what has happened before – is there a precedent? We might compare similar situations and look for historical parallels – are there patterns that repeat themselves in history and if so can we avoid the mistakes of the past? Countries which have prompted debate about foreign intervention more recently include Iraq, Afghanistan, Libya, Syria and Mali.

> **Task: think about**
>
> - If a country faces a humanitarian crisis (famine or genocide), how should the world react?
> - How far should our knowledge of history affect our judgement in this situation?

Knowledge of cause and effect

There may be an infinite number of causes of a single event. If a historian sets out to read every primary source that is relevant to the study of an event from the past, how far back does he or she need to go before claiming knowledge and understanding? There has to be a limit to the chain of causation as well as a limit to the sources that are thought to be relevant. Historians make a judgement about cause and effect relationships based on certain assumptions. These assumptions might include the idea that some causes are more significant than others, and that we can trace an event back to key evidentially supported causes. It is only with the benefit of hindsight that judgements about significant causes can be made.

The philosopher Blaise Pascal (1623–62) speculated that if the Egyptian Queen Cleopatra VII's nose had been shorter, the course of world history might have been different. At that time long noses were considered a beautiful feature symbolising strength of character. If Cleopatra's nose had been shorter, she might not have attracted the attention of Mark Antony and they might never have fallen in love. If so, they would not have fought together and lost against Octavian in the Battle of Actium in 31 BCE. If Octavian had not defeated them, then Rome might have remained a Republic, never become an Empire and might have fought off invasions successfully. Conceivably, had Cleopatra's nose been shorter, we might all still live under Roman rule and speak Latin and know nothing of Christianity.

These speculations might seem far-fetched but the point is that if you imagine taking out one event from the past you can speculate about what would have happened differently. This is known as **counter-factual history**. On a personal level we might imagine that there are chance happenings that seem to have significant far-reaching consequences: 'If I'd stayed at home and not gone out that day, I would never have met my future husband', 'If only I'd not sent that text, such and such would not have happened', and so on. With hindsight we can pick out small but significant factors that appear to shape the outcome of events.

What if Cleopatra's nose had been slightly shorter? If she had not been considered so beautiful, how might the course of Roman history have been different?

counter-factual history:
using imagination to speculate about 'what would have happened if . . .'

Compare the historical development of history with the historical development of other areas of knowledge. Think about the following:

- The task of the historian has been shaped by intellectual movements and key thinkers. What are the key intellectual movements and key thinkers that have contributed to our shared knowledge of history today? How does this compare with other areas of knowledge?

Task: activity

1. Outline and describe the methods used to gain historical knowledge.
2. What assumptions might historians make and if so do you think they are justified?
3. Explain what is meant by a historical fact and a historical explanation. Which do you think is more certain and why?

Personal knowledge

One reason why history is important to us as individuals is because we can learn from the mistakes of the past. The poem that opens Primo Levi's book *If This Is a Man* (1947) clearly indicates the moral purpose of remembering the Holocaust; his eyewitness account of his survival in Auschwitz points to the fact that the lessons learnt should be passed down to future generations, never to be forgotten.

The German scholar Leopold von Ranke was the founder of modern academic history. For him the purpose of history was to 'show what happened'. The historian G.R. Elton also defended the idea that history is a search for the objective truth about the past and that historical knowledge is out there waiting to be discovered.

A counter-argument was made by E.H. Carr, who challenged this traditional view of history. He wrote 'The belief in a hard core of historical facts existing objectively and independently of the historian is a preposterous fallacy, but one which is very hard to eradicate.'

In TOK there is a skill in reaching your own judgement having considered both sides of an argument. Your judgement needs to be supported with evidence and reasoning.

Task: think about

- Why might our personal knowledge of history be important to us?
- In what ways might individuals contribute to our shared historical knowledge?

Compare the links to personal knowledge in history with other areas of knowledge. Think about the following:

- the significance of history for you as an individual and its impact on your perspective
- your personal assumptions about history compared with your assumptions in other areas of knowledge.

Real-life situation

The assassination of US President J.F. Kennedy occurred in 1963. It is an event that was captured on film and broadcast on television around the world. We might think 'seeing is believing' but just because you see an event, does it mean your interpretation of it is necessarily true or accurate? Is it justified to assume that the eyewitness testimonies of the shooting of J.F. Kennedy are accurate and reliable as a source of knowledge? Our interpretation of events is shaped by the complex interrelationship between our sense perception, memory and imagination.

- To what extent do you think being an eyewitness to an event means that you know what happened?
- How far do you think our memory of events is reliable and accurate?

Do not waste words telling a long anecdote or an example that describes a historical event in detail. Focus your TOK writing on *analysis* of knowledge questions and give your own critical comment.

Knowledge question

- Can we be sure whether the historian has the same methodological rigour as the experimental scientist?

Presentation task

Consider giving a presentation on a knowledge question to do with our historical knowledge. Develop your own knowledge question from a real-life situation. An example of a real-life situation and a knowledge question that arises from it is shown on page 79. Make sure your chosen knowledge question is open-ended, explicitly to do with knowing or knowledge, and expressed in terms of TOK vocabulary.

Extended writing task

Write 500 words or more on one of the following questions:

1 To what extent does a historian's knowledge rely on particular ways of knowing?

2 Is our shared historical knowledge closer to our shared knowledge in science or literature?

3 How do we decide which events are historically significant?

Prescribed essay titles

1 What similarities and differences are there between historical and scientific explanations? (November 2009 and May 2010)

2 Compare and contrast our approach to knowledge about the past with our approach to knowledge about the future. (November 2008 and May 2009)

3 'History is always on the move, slowly eroding today's orthodoxy and making space for yesterday's heresy.' Discuss the extent to which this claim applies to history and at least one other area of knowledge. (November 2007 and May 2008)

Further reading and sources

Harris, Robert. 2006. *Imperium*. Hutchinson.
Hatcher, John. 2008. *The Black Death: A Personal History*. Da Capo Press.
Jaspers, Karl. 1953. *The Origin and Goal of History*. Routledge Revivals.
Levi, Primo. 1947. *If This Is a Man*. Orion Press. (English translation 1959.)
Lipstadt, Deborah. 1993. *Denying the Holocaust: The Growing Assault on Truth and Memory*. Penguin.
Rathbone, Mark. 2004. *'Gladstone, Disraeli and the Bulgarian Horrors.'* History Review. Available at: www.historytoday.com/mark-rathbone/gladstone-disraeli-and-bulgarian-horrors

Useful websites

www.birminghamhistorycenter.wordpress.com/2011/05/19/cleopatras-nose/
www.historytoday.com
www.history.ac.uk
www.niallferguson.com

9 Arts knowledge framework

Introduction

In this chapter we examine knowledge in the performing arts, the literary arts and the visual arts. The arts extend our experience and enrich our inner lives. By seeing films, reading novels, listening to music or going to art galleries we increase our personal knowledge and insight. We can learn about ourselves, our relationships and various cultures at different times. This chapter considers the role of emotion alongside the inner logic and rationality within the arts. It looks at the differences between **objective** and **subjective views of art**. It also explores how the arts make use of the broad range of ways of knowing available, including language, emotion, reason, perception and imagination.

objective view of art: the view that our judgement of art can be based on criteria and qualities that are independent of the observer
subjective view of art: the view that our judgements of art are based on personal preference

Task: think about

• What are your favourite film, poem, piece of music, novel and painting?
• Can you identify a link between your choices, or any cultural or gender bias?
• In what ways have your choices expanded your knowledge or insight?
• Do you think these insights count as personal or shared knowledge or both?

Think about the things that you know as a result of having read novels and poems, visited art galleries or seen theatre productions. Keep a record of them. You can use these examples in essays and presentations.

Use the knowledge framework to make comparisons and links between the arts and other areas of knowledge. Identifying similarities and differences between different areas of knowledge is one way to show your analytical skill.

A photograph of a nautilus shell. Is it beautiful? Is it art?

The Mandelbrot set forms a beautiful and intricate two-dimensional shape. The arts and mathematics both require creativity and imagination. What do you think are the connections and links between these two areas of knowledge?

Leela and Naresh are discussing knowledge in the arts.

Leela: How can the arts have anything to do with what we know? Surely music, painting and poems are there to be enjoyed and experienced? There's no knowledge involved.

Naresh: If you go into someone's house they're likely to have a picture up on their wall. We all know what looks good or sounds good. We all have aesthetic knowledge. It's a universal feature of what it is to be human.

Leela: Yes, but art and literature are just a matter of preference. Liking or disliking a painting or a poem is no different from liking or disliking sushi. Both are just a question of taste!

Naresh: Then why are some works of art and literature considered greater than others? Leonardo da Vinci's *Mona Lisa*, the plays and poetry of Shakespeare, and Beethoven's symphonies have stood the test of time. Even if we don't agree about what we like to look at or listen to, surely enduring art communicates some kind of universal and timeless truth?

Arts and culture

Among the earliest known artistic 'masterpieces' are the prehistoric cave paintings in Lascaux in France. Believed to possess 'outstanding universal value' and dating back around 1700 years, they are one of the UNESCO World Heritage sites. The instinct to create art has developed in all cultures: like language, the arts are universal. Some art forms are specific to particular cultures: the Japanese tea ceremony is an art form and a social activity; the Chinese dragon dance is a traditional part of Chinese culture; and the Keralan classical Indian dance-drama Kathakali is unique to southern India.

Compare the scope and applications of the arts with other areas of knowledge. Think about the following:

- The arts have a creative and imaginative motivation. How does this compare with other areas of knowledge? For example, the task of both an artist and a mathematician can be highly creative and imaginative, and the product of each arguably beautiful.
- How does the social function of the arts compare with that in other areas of knowledge?

The classical Keralan dance-drama, Kathakali, is deeply rooted in its Indian social and cultural context. Is it possible to know about the arts independently of their context?

Arts and commercial value

One morning in January 2007, a man on a subway platform in Washington, D.C. USA, played the violin. Many people passed him by in a hurry and failed to recognise who he was. He was one of the world's best violinists, Joshua Bell. Several nights earlier, he had performed in a concert, for which tickets were sold at a high price. The subway experiment was set up by the *Washington Post* to discover whether, in an everyday environment, people would recognise a famous musician's talent.

This was not intended to be a rigorous experiment but it makes us think about how our sense perception is affected by various factors. Art is not just about passively receiving sense data; music is not just about hearing. The way we judge art is heavily influenced by its context and setting, as well as our own expectations and priorities.

There is a social status associated with the creation and ownership of art, and art has a physical value. Jackson Pollock's painting *No. 5*, 1948 sold for $140 million in 2006 and Mark Rothko's *Orange, Red, Yellow* recently sold for $87 million. The British author J.K. Rowling made a fortune with her fictional creation of Harry Potter. If the creativity of individuals is driven by market forces, what are the implications? The market may be the final arbiter of the value of art, but is the value of art reducible to a sum of money?

The violinist Joshua Bell. What influences the value we place on art?

Arts and ethics

Should art ever be censored on ethical grounds? What is the relationship between the arts and ethics? The Greek philosopher Plato, in *The Republic*, written around 360 BCE, suggested that the arts should be censored by the state in people's best interests. Today the question remains unresolved about the ethical limits to our knowledge in the arts, and we debate issues of standards and taste. Artists explore the boundary between what is acceptable and unacceptable, often to make a point. For example, the artist Jill Greengrass photographed children who were upset and crying. Is this in poor taste or is it acceptable if it is called art?

There is an important relationship between the arts and education. Potentially the arts have a civilising effect; they broaden our perspective, and may open our eyes to social and ethical issues. The arts can communicate knowledge that will educate and inform. In the mid-nineteenth century the pre-Raphaelite painters in Britain were controversial for exposing the social ills of poverty, prostitution and hypocrisy. Their art set out to shed light on these social problems. Art that is considered shocking today might not be considered controversial in the future.

Art can touch on messy and complicated ethical themes; Shakespeare's play *Romeo and Juliet* deals with the stresses of family feuds and falling in love with someone who is considered unsuitable. The ethical dilemma that Juliet faces when she discovers that the man she has married, Romeo, has killed a member of her family reads like a plot from a television soap opera. People enjoy the thrill of a narrative based on an ethical dilemma.

> When you write about the arts, avoid making general claims that are difficult to support, such as 'The arts are just a matter of personal preference and contain no knowledge' or 'Art expresses the emotions of the artist and nothing else'.
>
> Think about the ways in which the arts contain more knowledge than we might first assume.

Task: activity

Consider these knowledge claims about art:

1 A work of art demonstrates skill.
2 A work of art imitates or copies nature.
3 A work of art expresses an emotion.
4 A work of art contains truth.

Match each of the examples below to one or more of the four claims about art.

a A photograph of a nautilus shell
b A painting entitled *The Scream* by Edvard Munch
c The classical Indian dance-drama, Kathakali, from Kerala
d Beethoven's Ninth Symphony
e Synchronised swimming performed at the Olympic Games
f Ballet performed as part of a circus act
g Michelangelo's paintings on the ceiling of the Vatican's Sistine Chapel
h A film that depicts martial arts using choreographed dance moves

---

Task: think about

- Which of the eight examples above do you consider to be art and which do you not consider to be art? On what grounds?
- Are any of these examples of 'great art'? Give your reasons.
- What is your own definition of art?
- What is the relationship between ethical values and the arts?

Compare the key concepts and language of the arts with other areas of knowledge. Think about the following:

- Many art forms do not use written language: dance, music and painting all use a non-verbal language. What role does language have in the arts and how does this compare with other areas of knowledge?
- What is the significance of form in the arts and how does this compare with other areas of knowledge?
- The arts use a number of key concepts, including creativity, imagination, form, language, fiction, truth, non-verbal language, metaphorical language, kitsch, mimesis, analysis, historical and cultural context, and paradigm. In what ways are these concepts similar or different in other areas of knowledge?

Methods used to produce knowledge in the arts

To explore the methods used to gain knowledge in the arts we will consider five ways of knowing: language, emotion, reason, perception and imagination.

Language

The poet, painter or musician has many tools and here we will consider language. The arts can communicate verbal knowledge, as in literature. Language in the arts can also be used metaphorically. In Shakespeare's play *Antony and Cleopatra*, Cleopatra nostalgically refers to her lost youth as her 'salad days'. This does not literally mean a time when she ate salad. Taken literally it makes no sense but taken as a metaphor she is remembering the freshness of her youth.

The artist Picasso once claimed that 'Art is a lie that brings us nearer to the truth.' When novelists use fictional characters and imagined events to communicate an experience, they are inventing within known artistic conventions. If the experience connects with us, the fictional story can persuade or convince us that we are learning something genuine about the real world. We can relate to the characters' experiences. We know not to interpret the language in the arts literally.

If you have ever written your own poetry or fiction you will know that finding the right words is difficult. The actor James Earl Jones observed that 'One of the hardest things in life is having words in your heart that you can't utter.'

Non-verbal language offers an alternative expression for our knowledge. The arts, including dance, music, painting and theatre such as mime, can communicate non-verbal knowledge: it is hard to put into words the feelings of listening to music such as Allegri's *'Miserere'*. The arts help us to express things that we cannot say directly, and it might not even be necessary to say what music communicates. This opens up the arts to communicating a wide range of knowledge.

The non-verbal arts have their own language. A performance of classical ballet fits a particular genre, convention and form. A performance of the American composer John Cage's piece *Four Minutes, Thirty Three Seconds* requires the audience to watch a 'performance' consisting of silence. There are a conventional audience, instruments on the stage, and the players dressed appropriately for a concert. Even though the performance takes place in silence it could be argued that it still relies on a type of non-verbal language. Images can also be considered a form of non-verbal language, for example **kitsch** or **mimesis**.

The (non-verbal) arts belong to one of the few areas of knowledge which can communicate knowledge without the spoken or written word. This is significant for TOK and invites you to consider what function language plays in the arts.

Emotion

Music has a very direct emotional impact and can affect our mood. If you listen to the fourth movement of Mahler's Fifth Symphony you might feel a range of emotions from sorrow to joy. Our feelings can also motivate us to create an artwork. The poet William Wordsworth described poetry as 'emotion recollected in tranquillity'. The arts can shape and change how we feel. An audience might respond emotionally to a work of art through its appeal to our shared emotions. Watching a performance of a tragedy on stage could move us to tears; a comedy might make us laugh.

The arts can give us a feeling of transcendence, a sense of a metaphorical window on another world. Bengal in India has a rich cultural and literary heritage. Rabindranath Tagore, a Bengali poet and polymath who was the first non-European to win the Nobel Prize in Literature in 1913, wrote a collection of poems entitled *Gitanjali*. With its spiritual and philosophical themes *Gitanjali* touches on universal emotions. But what moves one person emotionally might leave another feeling very little or nothing at all.

The arts can help us make sense of the world and give our lives meaning. They can help us feel more connected, understanding other people's emotions through empathy and being able to live vicariously through novels.

Reason

The evolutionary purpose of art and the precise role that the arts have played in terms of our survival is an important but disputed question. There is no Darwinian account of art that is agreed upon but there is a significant question here about the extent to which art is natural or cultural or both, and the implications of each position.

Our response to art is not just an automatic and unconscious instinct. We can stand back and rationally weigh up the content and form of a painting before arriving at a judgement. From a young age we can appreciate music, and the whole purpose of the arts is that they are accessible: anyone can enjoy them. Although judging art might seem more of a matter of the heart than the head, the arts are

---

non-verbal language: communication without words

kitsch: sentimental, clichéd or unoriginal art, for example a photo of a kitten on a greetings card

mimesis: the tradition of imitating or copying reality, for example a portrait which is a good likeness of the person

---

Metaphorical language is used in a non-literal sense. A simile compares two things using the words 'like' or 'as', for example 'My love is like a red rose'. A metaphor makes a comparison between two things more directly without using the words 'like' or 'as', for example 'My love is a red rose'.

Compare the methodology used in the arts with other areas of knowledge. Think about the following:

- Imagination and creativity are used to produce works in the performing, literary and visual arts. How is this similar or different in other areas of knowledge?
- The arts contain their own inner logic and coherence, and the creative process takes place within a framework using reason, structure and convention. For example, in poetry there are 14 lines in a sonnet and 17 syllables in a Japanese haiku.
- We assume conventions or genres to dictate artistic content to some degree.
- The arts use a method based on the concepts of form, structure, genre and context. How does this compare with other areas of knowledge?

If someone claims that this picture depicts a snow scene they are clearly wrong. As interpreters of the arts we need a degree of competence to make sound judgements. Is any interpretation of art acceptable?

open to rational criticism and interpretation. Reason provides a framework for the imagination.

In the arts there are rule systems for analysis. The use of literary devices in poetry and prose can be analysed as tools that create an artistic effect. Similarly the visual arts can be analysed using various concepts such as perspective, form, composition, colour, line, contrast and shadow. Prizes in the arts such as the Man Booker Prize, the Man Asian Literary Prize, the Pulitzer Prize and the Turner Prize indicate that we can make judgements about the arts based on criteria in which our reason and rationality are involved.

Perception

Our knowledge of the arts comes from viewing paintings, watching films, listening to music, and so on. Neuroaesthetics, developed by Semir Zeki, attempts to understand our response to art from the perspective of our shared neuroscientific knowledge. His work aims to understand what is happening in our brain when we look at art.

Dara Djavan Khoshdel set out to investigate the science behind the claim that some paintings are expensive because we respond to them emotionally. He investigated the emotional response of participants to the artwork of Graham Sutherland using a galvanic response monitor which measured their emotional response in relation to the small amounts of sweat they produced. He found that there was no link between the price of a painting and the participants' emotional response to it. His experiment indicated that if we know a painting is expensive it doesn't follow that we will be more moved emotionally by it.

The implications of this for our sense perception are significant. Some people

When we make judgements about the performing arts, the literary arts and the visual arts, which ways of knowing do you think are the most important and why?

might assume that our response to art is automatic, subconscious and instinctive. However, our response to artwork is not a purely instinctive response since it is shaped by various other factors including our expectations, our education and our cultural context. We actively interpret our sense perception of art in the light of these complex factors.

Imagination

Art can be a form of escapism where we can let our imagination loose. The arts enable us to travel inwardly and so expand our horizons. Reading literature from a range of cultures can widen our understanding of those cultures. We can also touch an experience of another person across time. Reading the poetry of Rumi (1207–73) gives us a great insight into the Persian spiritual wisdom of the past. By reading literature we can know more about our own mental narratives by comparing them with those of others, albeit invented. The American novelist Anne Tyler observed 'I write because I want more than one life; I insist on a wider selection. It's greed, plain and simple.'

Task: think about

- If it is the case that the arts can communicate in a way that language cannot, is it more appropriate to experience the arts rather than talk about them?
- What is the role of reason, emotion and sense perception in the arts?
- There are a number of approaches which aim to help us know about our appreciation of the arts from a scientific point of view. How might knowledge of our brain activity help or hinder our appreciation of the arts?
- Computer games entertain us with storytelling, music and pictures where we can experience a virtual world and another life. Do they expand or limit our imagination? Do you think that they are an art form and if so on what grounds?

Shared knowledge

Our idea of beauty changes over time and can vary across cultures. The curvaceous figures of European women in the eighteenth and nineteenth centuries were considered beautiful, yet today in some countries the fashion industry represents female beauty very differently. This raises the question: 'Does the fashion industry represent society's notions of beauty, or does it define beauty for society?'

On the one hand, art is very accessible since hearing music or seeing a sculpture is something we simply experience. On the other hand the arts are more esoteric. Knowing where Rothko fits into the history of art or where James Joyce's *Ulysses* fits into English literature requires much more knowledge and insight. To understand what is going on we need knowledge of the history, context and genre.

Knowing the context in which a work of art is produced can be the key to understanding its meaning. Gabriel Prokofiev composed *Concerto for Turntables and Orchestra* by combining his famous Russian grandfather Sergei Prokofiev's classical music traditions with the rhythms of modern club music. Our knowledge and insight into artworks of the present can be informed by knowledge of the historical development of an art form. Artworks can be consciously created in relation to what has come before; they can inform the present and point forwards to the future.

Compare the historical development of the arts with the historical development of other areas of knowledge. Think about the following:

- How far is the meaning of a work of art to be found in its historical and cultural context? Can we only make sense of an artwork if we know about the context in which it was created? How is this similar or different in other areas of knowledge?
- Which key intellectual movements and key thinkers have contributed to our shared knowledge of the arts today? How does this overlap and compare with other areas of knowledge?

Personal knowledge

The music you listen to and the books you read can define your identity. What we like to read or look at tells others something about the sort of person we are or the person we would like to become.

If you watch a production of Shakespeare's play *Macbeth* or the Indian adaptation *Maqbool* you will gain an insight into the devastating consequences of ambition and power. If you see Michelangelo's sculpture *Pietà* you might be overwhelmed by its realism. The arts help us to look at the world in new and original ways with fresh eyes. The Russian writer Viktor Shklovsky observed that 'Art makes the familiar strange so that it can be freshly perceived. To do this it presents its material in unexpected, even outlandish ways: the shock of the new.'

Compare the links to personal knowledge in the arts with other areas of knowledge. Think about the following:

- How might the arts expand your insights or deepen your awareness of yourself, of others or the society and world you live in?
- What is the significance of the arts for you as an individual? In what ways do the arts have an impact on your own perspective?
- How do individuals make a contribution to our shared knowledge in the arts?

Task: think about

- Technology gives rise to new art forms such as photography, film, computer art, computer games and computer music. What impact do you think technology is having and will have on the arts in the future?
- In what ways do the arts contribute to our understanding of ourselves or our world?
- For an individual to make a contribution to knowledge in the arts do you think they need to work within an established convention or challenge an existing convention?

Real-life situation

The Romanesco cauliflower is a beautiful, natural example of a volume fractal. A fractal is a pattern that repeats itself at ever smaller scales, so if you look at a tiny part of it, it looks the same as a larger part, but at a smaller scale. The closer you look, the more detail you see, like a world within a world. The mathematician Benoit Mandelbrot, in his book *The Fractal Geometry of Nature* (1983), first introduced and explained the concept of fractals and showed that they occur in nature.

Do you think that beauty has a mathematical basis?

Knowledge questions

- What is the role of emotion and reason in the arts?
- 'Those who create art have a moral duty.' Do you agree?

Presentation task

Consider giving a presentation on a knowledge question to do with the arts. Use a real-life situation from this chapter or think of your own. Make sure your knowledge question is open-ended, explicitly to do with knowing or knowledge and expressed in TOK vocabulary. The focus of your presentation should always be on an analysis of the knowledge question.

Extended writing task

Write 500 words or more on one of the following questions:

1 What, if anything, can we learn from the performing arts, the visual arts and the literary arts?

2 How do the methods used to gain knowledge in the arts compare with the methods used in one other area of knowledge?

3 Do we need to know the context in which an artwork was produced in order to claim that we have knowledge of that artwork?

4 What criteria need to be met before we are justified in claiming that we know something is great art?

Prescribed essay titles

1 'Art is a lie that brings us nearer to the truth' (Pablo Picasso). Evaluate this claim in relation to a specific art form (for example, visual arts, literature, theatre). (November 2010 and May 2011)

2 To what extent is truth different in mathematics, the arts and ethics? (November 2009 and May 2010)

3 '. . . we will always learn more about human life and human personality from novels than from scientific psychology' (Noam Chomsky). To what extent would you agree? (November 2007 and May 2008)

Further reading and sources

Nicholl, Charles. 2005. *Leonardo da Vinci: The Flights of the Mind.* Penguin.

Smith, Alison. *'Why were the Pre-Raphaelites so shocking?'* Tate blog, 30 August 2012. Available at: www.tate.org.uk/context-comment/blogs/why-were-pre-raphaelites-so-shocking

Warburton, Nigel. *'Can evolution explain aesthetics?'* Review of *The Art Instinct* by Dennis Dutton, Prospect Magazine. 26 April 2009. Available at: www.prospectmagazine.co.uk/magazine/canevolutionexplainaesthetics/

Weingarten, Gene. *'Pearls before breakfast: can one of the nation's great musicians cut through the fog of a D.C. rush hour?'* Washington Post, 8 April 2007. Available at: www.washingtonpost.com/wp-dyn/content/article/2007/04/04/AR2007040401721.html

Zeki, Semir. 2008. *Splendors and Miseries of the Brain: Love, Creativity, and the Quest for Human Happiness.* Wiley-Blackwell.

10 Ethics knowledge framework

The study of ethics is not a compulsory part of the IB curriculum but the learner profile assumes that 'acting in a principled way', which involves honesty, fairness and responsibility, is what IB students should do. Arguably ethics is the most important area of knowledge to you personally. What is a good life? How should we live our lives? What are the sources of our beliefs about right and wrong? Are there only personal standards of right and wrong or are there broader shared standards or even universal standards across different cultures? If there are such standards, what is their justification? In this chapter we are concerned with addressing these sorts of ethical knowledge questions. We will consider the basis for ethical judgements.

The statue *A Justiça* by Alfredo Ceschiatti, in front of the headquarters of the Supreme Court of Brazil. Can we observe right and wrong?

Sources of ethical knowledge

What's considered right and wrong varies between countries. Kissing in public is acceptable in the UK, but public displays of affection should be avoided in Singapore, Turkey and some other countries. It's very easy to assume that this area of knowledge is simply a matter of personal preference. People might feel strongly about the ethics of a number of national and international issues including world poverty, terrorism, climate change, oppressive political regimes, genetically modified crops, or the violation of human rights. If there is limited agreement between people, or if we can't make up our minds about ethical issues, it is sometimes assumed that ethics is all a matter of personal opinion.

You only need to break a rule in school or commit a crime to know that we are bound by rules and conventions everywhere. The IB rule that 'it is wrong to plagiarise someone else's work' carries with it an obligation not to do so. It follows that actions conform to or fail to conform to certain social or behavioural conventions. However, rules are not the same as morals. For example, some cultures regard it as 'immoral' for girls to speak to boys without a chaperone present. Homosexual relationships were once widely regarded as 'immoral' and are still regarded as immoral by some people.

On the level of personal knowledge, your source of right and wrong could include the standards you have been brought up with, or your individual **conscience**. Morality seems to be partly to do with social and cultural conventions. On the one hand, children are taught right and wrong by their parents so that they conform with the status quo. What we teach our children can become synonymous with what is right. On the other hand, good behaviour seems to be more than good manners. We mean something different from etiquette when we talk of right and wrong. Ethics is not just a matter of taste and convention.

You could opt to study 'theories and problems in ethics' formally as a philosophy option in Group 3. Ethics or moral philosophy explores human conduct and values. TOK ethics is concerned with whether or not we can have moral knowledge. It also concerns what is the best course of action under different ethical systems.

> **conscience**: our personal awareness of what is right and wrong; for example, our social conscience is our awareness of our ethical obligation and responsibility towards others

Task: think about

As you work through the activity that follows, reflect on the processes you use to arrive at ethical judgements.
- When you answer the questions, to what extent do you use reason, emotion or other factors when you make your judgements?
- When you answer the questions, in what ways does your perspective affect your judgement?

Task: activity

1 Which do you think is worse?
   a Being rude and unkind to someone
   b Being rude and unkind to someone behind their back but polite to their face
2 Which do you think is worse?
   a Killing one person deliberately
   b Killing two people by accident
   c Thinking about and planning how to kill someone but missing the opportunity to do so by accident
3 Which student deserves the severest punishment?
   a The student who deliberately steals someone else's mobile phone
   b The student who has been cyber-bullying another student
   c The student who is caught using the school photocopier for their own use without permission

Justification

The transatlantic slave trade in the eighteenth century may now be thought of as appalling or repugnant but some people considered it acceptable at that time. In the past, people watched Roman gladiators fight to the death for their own entertainment. **Ethical relativism** is the view that our sense of right and wrong depends on our cultural and historical context. However, within each historical setting or culture, the ethical view might be seen as absolute.

Considering the implications of ethical relativism, does it follow that anything is permitted? Arguably, it could follow that if female genital mutilation is acceptable in one cultural context, there is no way that a **relativist** can challenge it, since there are no objective grounds on which an action can be judged right or wrong. However, there might be grounds based on cultural convention. A relativist may claim that it is acceptable to wear a face covering, but not in France. In 2010 the

> **ethical relativism**: the view that there are no absolute standards of right and wrong; they vary and evolve differently across nations and cultures
>
> **relativist**: a person who thinks that there are no universal moral principles or absolutes since what we claim to know about right and wrong depends on our culture, country and place in history

French government banned face coverings in most public places in France, making it an offence for Muslim women to wear the burqa or niqab. This led to different views on the ethics of the ban, with those supporting it claiming that face coverings can cause security risks and those against the ban claiming that it limits individual rights. A relativist would argue that ethics are relative to the culture or the country you live in. This position might be argued for on the grounds that ethical judgements are **subjective**, that is, based on an individual's personal opinion.

There is an interesting relationship between ethics and **international-mindedness**. If we take a relativist position and promote tolerance of all practices in other cultures, what are the implications for ethics? Being internationally minded is not the same thing as being universally tolerant. It doesn't mean that we have to agree with practices in other cultures if we think that they are unethical. Someone might be internationally minded and be a supporter of Amnesty International, which opposes the abuse of human rights and is against the death penalty. Being internationally minded might influence how a student thinks and acts; they may become committed to a set of ethical values that could lead to action.

An alternative approach is to appeal to moral standards that are *universal*. You could accept that standards vary between cultures, but still claim that we can object to practices that seem to infringe the human rights of others. Amnesty International campaigns to uphold universal standards of human rights and abolish the use of torture in all circumstances. The UN Declaration of Human Rights assumes shared moral standards regardless of national and cultural differences. This approach claims that there are universal rules, or **moral absolutes**. This position might be argued for on the grounds that ethical judgements are **objective**; there are moral rules and standards that are in some sense independent of our personal preferences, perhaps with a natural or a divine basis.

What arguments might be used to support or oppose the right of Muslim women to wear the burqa or niqab?

subjective view of ethics: the idea that personal knowledge, our own thoughts, feelings, tastes and preferences are the basis of ethical judgements

international-mindedness: the mutual respect, understanding and interaction between different countries and cultures

moral absolutes: rules which apply universally, regardless of circumstances

objective view of ethics: the idea that there are moral truths 'out there' which could be natural or divine; for example, statements such as 'murder is wrong' are factual statements which are true or false in the same way that 'I have three books on my bookshelf' is true or false

---

> **Task: think about**
>
> - Think of examples of people who you would describe as internationally minded.
> - What attitudes and actions would you associate with someone who is internationally minded?
> - What is the distinction between an internationally minded person and an ethically minded person?
> - If you have helped others in need as part of CAS (creativity, action, service), reflect on the ways in which your involvement in CAS might have had an ethical dimension.

Ethics and international-mindedness

'to develop inquiring, knowledgeable and caring young people who help to create a better and more peaceful world through intercultural understanding and respect'

(IB Mission Statement)

We live in a world where we have many opportunities to appreciate and understand different cultures and ways of life. The boundaries between people and countries are ever closer, opening up the possibility for greater understanding. Having an international or global perspective may lead to certain values that have an ethical dimension such as tolerance and an attitude of respect for others. The IB Mission Statement identifies values and attitudes that have an ethical dimension.

The United Nations exists to promote peace, respect and good relationships between different countries and cultures, and its Secretary General, Ban Ki-moon, commented that 'Now, more than ever, we need to connect the dots between climate, poverty, energy, food and water. These issues cannot be addressed in isolation.' Having an education which promotes an international perspective might lead to thinking about our ethical responsibility to address these sorts of local and global challenges.

Task: activity

1   How do we defend our ethical values? Think about what sorts of *evidence*, *reasons* and *arguments* we use. In pairs, write a short speech that supports or opposes one of the following ethical issues: abortion, the death penalty, wearing the burqa, or public displays of affection.
2   Write a critical analysis of your speech.
    a   Which of your arguments do you think is strongest and why?
    b   Which of your arguments do you think is weakest and why?
    c   What values are you assuming your listeners have?
    d   If everyone in the world were in agreement with what you say in your speech, how would the world be different?

Task: think about

Here are some unresolved questions in ethics:
- How are moral judgements similar to or different from other types of judgement?
- Should we act in our own self-interest or in the interest of others?
- Do we invent or discover moral values?
- Are human rights universal or culturally relative?
- Is our sense of right and wrong something we are born with or something we have been taught, or both?
- Is it possible to measure good and bad behaviour?
- Is an action right or wrong because of its consequences?
- Can a good person do a bad thing and vice versa?
- Are there moral facts? If so, on what grounds might you establish these facts?

Compare the key concepts and language of ethics with other areas of knowledge. Think about the following:

- What is distinctive about the role of ethical language? What is the purpose of ethical language and how does this compare with the way language is used in other areas of knowledge?
- In ethics the character of an action can be judged by a number of key concepts, including virtue, intention, duty and consequence. How do these key concepts compare with other areas of knowledge?

Ethical language and key concepts

A statement of fact is 'All IB students study TOK.' A statement of value is 'All IB students *should* act in a principled way.' Ethics addresses these statements of value, to do with the *shoulds* and *should nots*, the *oughts* and *ought nots*. Ethical values are concerned with practical obligations to act in a particular way. The language we use seems secondary to the action itself. The saying 'actions speak louder than words' seems to apply to ethics, since moral language carries with it the requirement to act.

'With great power comes great responsibility.' (Voltaire)
Do you think that higher ethical standards are expected of people who have great responsibility?

Consider these examples. Which of them are statements of fact and which are statements of value?

1 All IB students are required to write an Extended Essay.
2 All IB students are expected to be principled and honest.
3 Serving the local community is a good thing.
4 Passing off someone else's work as your own is a definition of plagiarism.
5 CAS involves 150 hours of work.
6 Scientists, historians and religious leaders have a moral duty.
7 All IBDP students are advised to choose six subjects.
8 It is wrong to copy part of someone else's essay and hand the work in as if it is your own.

Methods used to produce knowledge

We will consider the methods used to gain knowledge in ethics, making links with methods used in other areas of knowledge and exploring these in relation to reason, emotion and faith.

Reason

When you experience the feeling that something is wrong there may be a good reason to justify that feeling. If you feel angry, it may be that an injustice has been done. There can be a rational basis to our feelings of right and wrong.

Reason can be used to argue from **general moral principles** to particular examples. For example, 'right speech' is one of the principles of the Buddhist Noble Eightfold Path. If someone accepts this general principle, they might argue that it is wrong to gossip or speak in a negative way about other people.

There may be different cultural approaches to forming a queue but if I believe that it is right to stand in a queue for my lunch it would be wrong for me as an individual to push in at the front of the queue. It would be unreasonable to jump a queue because if everyone did this there would be chaos with everyone pushing in. The chaos wouldn't necessarily be unethical, however, and could simply be classed as annoying. Nevertheless, it's not reasonable to think that there should be one rule for me and another rule for everyone else.

Potentially there is a rational basis for ethics and you might argue that something is right or wrong on rational grounds. Many people have argued that morality has a solid basis in the shared needs of physical existence. There are biological explanations for behaviour that is

general moral principle: a fundamental ethical proposition, rule or belief that a person might live by, such as the Golden Rule, 'treat others as you would like to be treated'

It would be wrong for a scientist to ignore data that falsifies their hypothesis. How do values, standards and conventions shape different areas of knowledge?

selfish or the opposite, altruistic. There are good reasons why we might behave collaboratively and cooperatively. While we might think of 'good' people as those who are public spirited, selfless and empathetic, there may be a biological basis for their behaviour. Our social survival is related to our reputation and the way we behave.

We might use reason to put forward arguments to defend our position on a particular ethical issue. For example, is it ethical to help someone die? Voluntary euthanasia is an issue that arises when a person who is seriously ill or has a terminal illness with no chance of recovery requests another person to help them to die. Euthanasia is different from suicide because someone else is helping the person die. It is also distinct from murder because it is requested by the ill person. Someone might argue that it is ethical if it is what the person has requested and it would minimise their suffering. On the other hand, a course of action that results in someone's death is considered unethical and illegal in many countries, including the UK. It is, however, legal under some circumstances in countries such as Switzerland, the Netherlands and some states in Australia and the USA.

It might be argued that euthanasia is unethical because even if the patient requests it, it involves someone else, usually a doctor, helping them die. This is against the Hippocratic Oath, an agreement that doctors make when they enter the profession, that they are committed to life and will not harm their patients. This argument assumes the inherent value of human life and the ethical responsibility of doctors. Many of the arguments against voluntary euthanasia boil down to the principle that life should be preserved at all costs, whereas arguments for voluntary euthanasia are often based on the principle that individuals have the right to choose how and when they die.

People are unlikely to agree on all matters of ethical principle, but we might make use of facts to support an argument. A disagreement between two people about whether it is possible to regulate euthanasia might be resolved by looking at the empirical evidence from countries where it is legal. Similarly we might look at the evidence behind the argument that legalising euthanasia would expose vulnerable people to feel pressured to end their lives.

Task: think about

Do you think it is morally right to protect our children because this is key to our survival as a species?

Compare the methodology used to gain knowledge in ethics with other areas of knowledge. Think about the following:

- Are there any ethical facts?
- Ethical decisions are made on a personal level according to what we think is right or wrong. How does this compare with judgements made in other areas of knowledge?
- Is there a method for gaining ethical knowledge?
- How might facts be relevant to the ethical judgements we make?

Emotion

How we feel seems to influence our judgement of right and wrong. We can instantly feel repulsion to horrific acts. Our moral knowledge might be based on a gut feeling, an intuition that enables us to know the difference between right and wrong.

Some people think the use of animal experiments in the development of pharmaceutical drugs is intuitively wrong. You might be able to put forward arguments based on reason to support or oppose the use of animal experiments independently of how you feel about it. Although we may have an intuitive sense of right and wrong, the question here is, what would be a reliable *measure* of right and wrong?

When you write about ethics in TOK, think in terms of:

- How do I know what is right or wrong?
- What is the source of my beliefs about right and wrong?
- When I make an ethical judgement, which ways of knowing am I making use of and how?
- Who might disagree with me and why?
- What are the different cultural and historical perspectives?

Real–life situation

In the early 1990s the controversial 'performance' artist Rick Gibson took 'Sniffy the Rat' from a pet shop, where he might have been sold as live snake food. Gibson set up a device to crush the rat with a large weight and make an artwork with the remains. The rat was rescued by activists, who felt that what Gibson had planned was wrong, but Gibson's point was to invite a discussion about the ethics of killing animals. If the rat had been sold as live snake food, it would have faced inevitable death.

Faith

The notion of God as the source of moral knowledge can inspire religious believers to have faith in a God-given code of ethics or divine commands. Religious knowledge systems contain codes for living that set out guidelines for behaviour.

The Golden Rule has been around since the time of Confucius. It is the idea that it is right to treat others as we would like to be treated ourselves. The negative version of the rule follows that it is wrong to treat others in a way that you would not like to be treated yourself. A version of it appears in Leviticus 19:18 in the Bible. Jesus also reiterated it in the New Testament.

However, it doesn't follow that those who belong to a religion necessarily have a better set of moral values or privileged access to ethics since faith and morality are distinct. Similarly many religions recognise that being religious isn't the same as being moral. The book of James in the Bible suggests that true religion involves concern for orphans and widows. There's a distinction between how we live and what we believe. Arguably how we live is more important than what we believe.

The Dalai Lama is the spiritual spiritual leader of Tibetan Buddhists. To what extent do you think there are differences between religious and non-religious views of ethics?

Task: think about

- Does reasoning seem like a reliable method for gaining ethical knowledge?
- To what extent do you think it is rational to be good? Give examples.
- Is an action good if it makes me and other people feel happy? Give examples.
- What do you think is more important: faith, belief or how we act?

Task: activity

1 Construct an argument either for or against voluntary euthanasia or a related ethical issue. Think of around three points for your case.
   • What are the *facts* that might support your argument?
   • What are the *principles* you will use to support your argument?
   You may find the following website useful as a resource: www.bbc.co.uk/ethics/euthanasia/
2 What does the activity above tell you about the nature of ethical arguments? Make a list of key points.

Theories

The fourth part of the knowledge framework encourages you to think about how ethics has been shaped by key historical developments. It is useful to have an awareness of how our ethical knowledge might be shaped by the contribution of key thinkers and their ethical theories.

One of the most important questions in life is 'What sort of person should I be?' This question is there for you to answer, and ethics offers a framework. In ethics there are at least three main categories of theory: **deontological theories**, **consequentialist theories** and **virtue ethics**. The first two are theories about ethical actions: deontological theories look 'behind' an action to its motives and intentions, whereas consequentialist theories look 'beyond' an action to its outcomes and consequences.

Theories might provide the source or the justification for what we think is right: 'I did this because I thought it was my duty to do so' or 'I did this because I thought that the outcome would benefit others.' In addition, ethical theories can provide a framework for generating ethical principles.

Deontological theories

An action might be judged right or wrong on deontological grounds if you intend good to come from it, and this might seem like a fair and reasonable measure of ethical actions. However, there may be scenarios you can think of where you might act unethically without intending to do so. For example, someone might park a car and forget to put the hand brake on, so that the car rolls back and causes the death of a passer-by. Judging the ethics of an action according to a person's intentions alone seems to be problematic. We have all done things that have led to unintended consequences. There may also be problems with knowing another person's true intentions or even assessing accurately our own motives.

Immanuel Kant's deontological theory of ethics says that reason alone can determine whether an action is right or wrong. By universalising an action, asking 'What if everybody did that?', a person can discover if their actions are reasonable. Moreover, since every person is a moral agent and can make moral decisions, it is our duty to treat everyone with the respect that we expect for ourselves. There is a clear rational basis to ethics but there is a degree of imagination required: a sense of how things would be if everyone acted in this way. It follows that our private and public lives should be governed equally by the requirement to do our duty.

deontological theories: measure whether an action is right or wrong by considering the nature of the action itself, the motivation or the intention behind it

consequentialist theories: measure whether an action is right or wrong on the basis of the result, outcome or consequence of the action

virtue ethics: considers a person's character, and what it is to be a good person

Consequentialist theories

According to a different measure, an action might be judged right or wrong on consequentialist grounds if my actions produce a good outcome or result. This might seem like a reasonable measure of ethical actions. However, the measure of outcomes is problematic: does someone consider the consequences of the action from their own perspective or the perspective of others, and how do we measure the benefit arising from the action? There may be scenarios you can think of where unethical actions could be 'justified' on the grounds of the consequences of the action: taking from the rich to give to the poor, or harming one person in order to save the lives of ten people. Considering the consequences alone doesn't seem to provide a reliable measure of whether or not an action is ethical.

Utilitarianism is a consequentialist theory of ethics that suggests that an action is ethical if it produces certain consequences or results. Utilitarianism, like other consequentialist theories, measures the moral worth of an action by its effects. An act is good if it increases pleasure or happiness, and bad if it increases pain or suffering. This measurement can be applied to individual actions (act-utilitarianism) or to general rules of behaviour (rule-utilitarianism). A world in which everyone follows the rule not to steal, for example, might arguably be a happier world. Judging an action's likely outcome and consequences depends on imagining and anticipating the foreseeable consequences and weighing up which would be more favourable.

British philosopher Philippa Foot's original version of an ethical dilemma known as the trolley problem: a person is driving a tram that is out of control and can only be steered from one track onto another. If the driver continues on the track ahead, five people will be killed. There is another track with one person who would die. What is the right thing for the driver to do?

A variation of the dilemma is that a passer-by can switch a lever which will change the course of the trolley.

Another variation is where the same trolley is hurtling towards five people lying on a train track. A man is standing on a bridge and if you push him his mass will stop the trolley. In all scenarios the outcome is the same; you may sacrifice one person to save the lives of five others. What is the ethical difference between switching the lever and pushing the man? What is the right thing to do?

Task: think about

Look at the trolley dilemma. For more examples of ethical dilemmas, look at the website of American political philosopher Michael Sandel: www.justiceharvard.org
- How might ethical theories help you decide what the right course of action is?
- What do you think is the right thing to do in this situation?
- When you make ethical judgements, which ways of knowing are you making use of and how?
- How do you arrive at a judgement?

Virtue ethics

Virtue ethics is about the ethical *character* of people rather than ethical actions. The approach of virtue ethics first proposed by Aristotle does not ask whether actions are right or wrong, but asks instead whether people are virtuous. We can spot good and bad character traits in ourselves and others. A good life is one that is lived according to virtue: that is, following habits and attitudes that will lead to a desired goal. For example, a student who wants to do well will cultivate the habits of hard work and concentration, and whatever they do with these virtues will bring them closer to success. A lazy and distracted student on the other hand will not succeed, because these are vices.

Task: think about

- What are the best and worst actions that you have ever done?
- What features made these actions either wrong or right? The action itself, the consequences or something else?
- Should we conform to existing ethical codes for living or invent our own ethical rules?
- To what extent are ethical theories a reliable guide to what is right?
- What would you include in a list of ethical virtues and why?

Personal knowledge

It seems remarkable to think that NASA is looking at how we can use our mathematical and scientific knowledge to plan future space travel to the planet Mars, and yet when it comes to ethics we have no certain answers. We may, however, make a judgement about the ethics of putting resources into space travel.

Despite the fact that ethics is highly personal, and ethical issues are open to personal interpretation, ethics is still arguably one of the most important areas of knowledge on an individual level. In terms of our personal knowledge, ethics is about how we live, how we should act, what we think is fair, and what type of people we would like to become. Of all the areas of knowledge, ethics has the biggest implications for us as people and our personal judgement is the key.

Real-life situation

Examples of ethical issues with a global or international perspective include the work being done by governments and non-governmental organisations (NGOs) to address problems such as:
- world poverty and the fact that there are 1.4 billion people in the world living in extreme poverty, on less than $1.25 a day: www.globalpovertyproject.com/pages/presentation
- the environment, global warming and Greenland's melting ice sheet: www.greenpeace.org/international/en/
- saving the lives of children through vaccinations and the work of UNICEF and its partners: www.unicef.org/

Compare the links to personal knowledge in ethics with other areas of knowledge. Think about the following:
- the implications of accepting a shared or universal code of ethics for you as an individual
- how you might make a contribution to shared ethical knowledge
- whether there are any experts on ethics.

Compare the historical development of ethics with the historical development of other areas of knowledge. Think about the following:
- how ethics has been shaped by intellectual movements and key thinkers
- how ethical theories compare with theories in other areas of knowledge.

Knowledge question

- On what grounds can we justify ethical judgements made in two different areas of knowledge?

Presentation task

Consider giving a presentation on a knowledge question to do with ethics. Use a contemporary ethical issue with a global or international perspective, such as one of the examples on page 99, or develop your own knowledge question from another real-life situation. Make sure your knowledge question is open-ended, explicitly to do with knowing or knowledge, comparative and expressed in TOK vocabulary. The focus of your presentation should always be on the analysis of a knowledge question.

Extended writing task

Write 500 words or more on one of the following questions:

1 In what ways do ethical theories expand or limit my knowledge of what is right and wrong and how do they compare with theories in other areas of knowledge?

2 Can we know for certain what is right and wrong?

3 The philosopher Jean-Paul Sartre observed that everything has been discovered except how to live. To what extent do you agree?

4 'There is nothing either good or bad, but thinking makes it so.' (Shakespeare, *Hamlet*, Act II, Scene ii) To what extent do you agree?

Prescribed essay titles

1 'Moral wisdom seems to be as little connected to knowledge of ethical theory as playing good tennis is to knowledge of physics' (Emrys Westacott). To what extent should our actions be guided by our theories in ethics and elsewhere? (November 2008 and May 2009)

2 Are reason and emotion equally necessary in justifying moral decisions? (November 2007 and May 2008)

3 Consider the extent to which knowledge questions in ethics are similar to those in at least one other area of knowledge. (November 2010 and May 2011)

Further reading and sources

Ban, Ki-moon. Remarks at UNFCCC, 7 December 2010. Available at:
    www.un.org/en/globalissues/briefingpapers/youth/quotes.shtml
Blackburn, Simon. 2001. *Being Good: A Short Introduction to Ethics*. Oxford University Press.
Glover, Jonathan. 1977. *Causing Death and Saving Lives: The Moral Problems of Abortion, Infanticide, Suicide, Euthanasia, Capital Punishment, War, and Other Life-or-Death Choices*. Penguin
Mackie, J.L. 1977. *Ethics: Inventing Right and Wrong*. Penguin.
Singer, Peter. 1986. *Applied Ethics: Oxford Readings in Philosophy*. Oxford University Press.
United Nations, The Universal Declaration of Human Rights. Available at:
    www.un.org/en/documents/udhr/index.shtml
Vardy, Peter, and Grosch, Paul. 1994. *The Puzzle of Ethics*. Fount.

11 Religious knowledge framework

Introduction

Religious knowledge is perhaps the most contentious of all areas of knowledge. There are some people who would claim that there is no such thing, while there are others who regard their religious knowledge as the most certain of the truths that they hold.

In this chapter we will look at religious knowledge, the ways in which people arrive at it, and some of the knowledge questions that arise.

"How much do you know?
And how much do you just suspect?"

What is religious knowledge?

In Unit 1 we found that for something to be knowledge it has to satisfy at least some of these criteria:

- something for which there is persuasive evidence or rational argument
- something accepted by a large body of people
- something we would act upon
- something that might cause us to change our behaviour
- something that forms a part of a larger body of claims that are held to be true.

Religious traditions constitute an array of knowledge. Some of this knowledge will be about the origins of the religion, its traditions and artefacts, history of interpretation, ethical beliefs, or rites, rituals and festivals. This type of knowledge is similar to knowledge in history and the humanities. A great deal of it will be historical in nature, and its justification may be subject to the same criteria as any historical knowledge.

Such knowledge is usually widely accepted outside the religious tradition as well as by believers. For example, many people accept the historicity of Siddhartha Gautama, Jesus of Nazareth and Muhammad without being Buddhists, Christians or Muslims. Many people of different religions, including people with no religion, accept that these leaders were real men who lived in particular places and times, just as they accept that Julius Caesar, Asoka and Aristotle were real people who lived in the past.

Compare the links to personal knowledge in religious knowledge with other areas of knowledge. Think about the following:

- the significance of religion for you as an individual and its impact on your perspective
- your personal assumptions about religion compared with your assumptions in other areas of knowledge
- how individuals might make a contribution to shared religious knowledge
- what it means to be an expert in a religious knowledge system.

Task: think about

Consider the claims 'Buddha lived in the sixth century BCE', 'Buddha was the son of a very rich man', 'Buddha meditated for years under a Bodhi tree', 'Buddha achieved enlightenment', 'Buddha is an avatar of Vishnu', 'Hindus believe that Buddha is an avatar of Vishnu'.
- Do these claims all constitute knowledge?
- If so, is all the knowledge they represent of the same kind?
- Which of these claims are historical?

⭐ Do not write about religion as if all religions are the same. Not all religions have identifiable founding figures, not all have holy scriptures, not all have gods, not all have creeds, and not all have beliefs about an afterlife or reincarnation.

Religious knowledge is more than knowledge about the origins and practices of religions. It also involves claims about the significance of the religion and it is here that most of the contention arises. Even though non-believers may accept the historicity of Siddhartha Gautama, Jesus of Nazareth and Muhammad, it is usually only members of Buddhist, Christian and Muslim religious communities respectively who treat their religious claims as knowledge. Moreover, even within a single religious tradition, believers will differ in which claims they accept and how they interpret and understand the knowledge claims they assent to. Examples of religious claims include:

- Jesus Christ is the Son of God. (Christianity)
- Observing the five pillars of Islam is necessary to secure a place in heaven. (Islam)
- The Noble Eightfold Path is the way to the cessation of suffering. (Buddhism)
- The Jade Emperor governs the realm of the mortals. (Taoism)

Believers may claim such statements from their own religion as things that they know, but it is unlikely that many non-believers would regard these statements as true. These are knowledge claims based on faith. Believers may regard them as justified true beliefs (to use a definition of knowledge from Unit 1) and therefore as religious knowledge, but non-believers may dismiss them as both unjustified and untrue.

Task: think about

There are some religious claims that may ring true for many believers of different religions and non-believers alike. One example might be 'human life is valuable'.
- Can you think of others?
- Explain whether or not you would regard such claims as knowledge.

Religious language

Religion is a difficult area of knowledge to discuss, not least because the ways in which words are used when discussing religious ideas are often different from the ways in which the same words are used in other contexts. For example, when people claim 'polar bears exist' they base the claim on quite different criteria from those they use when they claim 'God exists'. Before we can decide whether the claim 'God exists' is justified, we have to know what we mean by the words *God* and *exists*.

The different use of words can have some very strange consequences. Take, for example, four people, two of who claim 'God exists', and two of whom claim 'God does not exist'.

Religious reference

If Mark and Sameera claim 'God exists', we may think they agree with each other. But Mark might believe God to be the entire universe (pantheism) and Sameera might believe God to be something other than the universe (theism). What they mean by what they say is very different.

Similarly Nisha and Carlos might both claim 'God does not exist' and also be thought to agree with each other. But Nisha may believe there is no God, whether part of the universe or not, and Carlos might believe in a God who is other than the universe and has no physical existence. If this were the case, Carlos would be much more in agreement with Sameera than Nisha, despite making an apparently contradictory claim.

> ### Task: think about
>
> How important is it that we know what a word refers to before we can be said to know anything about it?

Of course there are multiple ways people can understand the words *God* and *exist* and so a lot of religious discourse is about attempting to clarify meanings and reach common understandings, often using metaphorical language. But metaphorical language can itself create misunderstandings, with some people interpreting as literal what is meant as metaphorical and vice versa. To what extent can those outside a religious tradition really understand its key ideas when even those within the religious tradition do not have a common understanding about them?

ⓘ Theism and pantheism are only two ways of thinking about who or what God is. There are others such as panentheism and deism that you might like to research.

ⓘ In his book *Systematic Theology I*, Christian theologian Paul Tillich argued: 'God does not exist. He is being itself beyond essence and existence. Therefore to argue that God exists is to deny him.' In other words, he argues that if we believe in God, we should say that God *does not* exist. What do you think?

★ Be careful in your use of language. Do not slide from one definition of a key word to another without explaining that you intend to do so and your reasons for it.

Even when we speak a common language, our words may be misunderstood.

Where does religious knowledge come from?

Let us put aside the issue of language and assume for now that we can all agree on what is meant when someone makes a claim to have religious knowledge. Where does this knowledge come from?

Direct revelation including mystical experiences

Direct revelation (or special revelation) is when God is claimed to have revealed Godself to a person. Examples of this include the revelation of the Ten Commandments to Moses and the revelation of the Qur'an to Muhammad.

© Randy Glasbergen
www.glasbergen.com

"Wireless communication is nothing new. I've been praying for 75 years!"

Many people of different theistic religious traditions believe that God can communicate with them directly, for example through dreams and visions, or through an inner voice during prayer and meditation. Most of the world's religions have mystical traditions in which believers feel oneness with the divine or a profound and powerful loss of self. By their nature, mystical experiences cannot be shared, they have to be experienced, but poetry, metaphor, koans and paradoxes are some of the ways in which mystics try to communicate their own experiences to others.

Many Hindus believe God may be revealed through *darshan* (the Sanskrit word for seeing) in which God sees and is seen by the worshipper. As in English, the word carries the double meaning of visually seeing and understanding, thus a pious Hindu may experience a revelatory sense of understanding by looking at a *murti* (the representation of a god).

Emotion plays a significant role in direct revelation because the person who has a revelatory experience often claims to recognise the revelation by the experience of accompanying emotional changes such as a sense of awe, love, peace, or inner calm. The strong emotional connections that people have with their religious beliefs are one of the reasons why religion is such a sensitive area. When discussing religion it is always important to be willing to *listen* to different points of view, even though we may not agree with them. We cannot expect others to respect our beliefs if we do not respect theirs.

Compare the methodology used to gain knowledge in religions with methodologies used other areas of knowledge. Think about the following:

- A religious and historical fact might be that Siddhartha Gautama became known as the Buddha. A religious explanation of this transition would require religious interpretations of the evidence. How might religious explanations compare with explanations in other areas of knowledge?
- Religious scholars assume that knowledge from the past is reliable and that direct revelation is possible. How might assumptions behind religious knowledge systems compare with assumptions made in other areas of knowledge?

Task: think about

- What is the difference between hearing a voice and hearing 'a voice in your head'?
- What ways of knowing might play a part in direct revelation and how reliable are they?
- How can we know with certainty if someone has had a direct revelation?
- Why might it seem easier to believe in direct revelations that were claimed to have happened hundreds of years ago than those that are claimed to have happened recently?

Indirect revelation

Indirect revelation is when people treat records of special revelations received by others as authoritative. For example, the Adi Granth, the Qur'an and the Vedas are believed to be revealed or inspired, and therefore regarded as authoritative by Sikhs, Muslims and Hindus respectively. Scriptures may also be understood to record the memories of revelatory experiences and miracles as well as activities and beliefs of the early followers, thus providing current believers with knowledge about early teachings and practices. Although these scriptures may be regarded by believers as *directly revealed*, when the believer reads the texts for inspiration from them, that inspiration is called *indirect revelation*.

> **Task: think about**
>
> - Even if we accept that direct revelations have occurred, how can we be certain that the surviving compilations of texts accurately represent what was revealed?
> - In many ancient religions the teachings have passed from one generation to the next orally. It is often many years after the revelatory events that the teachings have been written down. What may have been lost or added along the way, by whom and why? How can we know?
> - Even the most careful translations from one language to another create changes to meaning. Reading a text in its original language may give some advantage but language is a dynamic system and the use of words changes over time. How then, can we be sure when reading ancient texts that they meant then what we think they mean now?

Miracles

Miracles are a feature of many religions and they are often used to justify belief in God, gods, or other supernatural entities, but how they are understood varies widely. Some people regard miracles as seemingly impossible events that interrupt the laws of nature and are caused by some kind of supernatural being; others argue that miracles are evidence of a supernatural being working within the laws of nature (even if they involve natural laws that we have not yet discovered).

For many people an unlikely beneficial event such as recovery from a life-threatening illness may be considered a miracle; others may regard even common natural events as miraculous, for example 'the miracle of birth'.

> **Task: think about**
>
> - To what extent are miracles reasonable?
> - To what extent is belief in miracles compatible with our scientific knowledge?
> - What evidence would you need to be persuaded that a miracle had happened:
>   a in the past as reported by others
>   b in the present as reported by others
>   c in your own experience?
> - What difference does our definition of *miracle* make to our willingness to accept that a miracle has occurred?
> - How can we know whether **spiritual experiences** are a connection with the divine (however that might be conceived) or simply strong emotional responses?

spiritual experiences: experiences such as feelings of awe or oneness with the universe that a person might experience when doing things such as looking at a breathtaking landscape, serving others, or practising meditation or yoga

Religious authorities

Most established religions have religious authorities: priests, imams, mufti, ayatollahs, lamas, shamans, Brahmin, rabbis, monks, theologians or others. One of the functions of these authorities is to interpret the teachings and traditions of their religion for lay people, and to determine which variations of interpretation are permissible, and which are to be regarded as heretical. Religious authorities also have some responsibility for discerning which accounts of direct revelation and miracles are authentic. In other words, they often decide what counts as religious knowledge and what does not.

Some religious authorities have a great deal of political power as well as religious influence. Many people have been persecuted, excluded from society or even killed for having opinions that differ from those of religious authorities (heresy) or for abandoning their religious beliefs (apostasy).

Apostasy is still a capital offence in some parts of the world. This means that people can receive the death penalty for deciding that they no longer believe in their religion.

Task: think about

Task: think about

- On what basis is the authority of a religious leader established?
- What ways of knowing must we use to distinguish sincere religious leaders from charlatans and powerseekers?
- To what extent does the popularity of an authority legitimise that authority?
- Why might some societies feel the need to kill or expel heretics and apostates?

Compare the historical development of religious knowledge systems with the historical development of other areas of knowledge. Think about the following:

- The task of religious scholars has been shaped by intellectual movements and key thinkers. Who are the key thinkers who have contributed to our shared knowledge of religions today?
- How have intellectual movements shaped our knowledge and understanding of religious knowledge systems? How does their influence on religious knowledge systems compare with their influence on other areas of knowledge?

Tradition

Religious tradition might be regarded as a faith community's memory. It is the momentum of the beliefs, practices and interpretations of the community of believers as they are passed down from one generation to the next. It is not a static thing; it evolves from and draws upon the full interpretative and ritualistic history of a religion.

Typically religious traditions vary from one culture to another despite common origins. For example, the forms of Buddhism practised in Sri Lanka tend to be markedly different from those practised in China or Japan. Within most of the world's major religions there are numerous traditions. These may sometimes differ quite significantly from each other in their religious practices and in their acceptance and interpretation of religious teachings.

Task: think about

- How do traditions change and grow? Is this the same as saying they progress?
- What might religious progress look like?
- What is your response to the ways in which the same religion can differ so greatly across time and place?
- On what basis would you accept that truths based on events that happened hundreds or thousands of years ago should remain unchanged and unchallenged in the present?

Ways of knowing in religion

All ways of knowing may be used when developing or accepting religious knowledge. We have already considered the importance of language, and we have seen how sense perception and emotion play their parts in whether we recognise revelations and miracles. Here we will look at three more ways of knowing that are particularly important in determining religious knowledge.

Reason

It may be surprising to discover that reason is regarded as an important feature of theology in many of the world's theistic (god-based) religions, as well as in nontheistic religions (such as Jainism, Buddhism and Confucianism) which are often philosophical in nature. Theologians often make reasoned arguments from religious axioms, which are usually derived from one or more of the knowledge sources above. Of course, as you have discovered, no matter how logical the argument, the validity of any conclusion reached can only be as reliable as the validity of the axioms on which it is based.

There have also been attempts to argue the existence of God without having to rely upon experiential evidence. St Anselm's ontological argument is a famous example of an attempt to prove the existence of God using logic.

Anselm's ontological argument

a God is the greatest being we can imagine.

b The idea of God exists in the mind.

c It is greater to exist in reality than to exist only in the mind.

d If God exists only in the mind, then we can conceive of a greater being – that which exists in reality.

e We cannot conceive of a being greater than God, therefore God must exist in reality.

Pascal's wager

Pascal's wager is an argument for living as if God exists, based on probability. His idea can be summed up as follows: If we bet that God exists (and live accordingly) and we are right, we will get the rewards of heaven. If we are wrong, we do not lose anything. However, if we bet that God does not exist and we are right, we do not gain anything. But if we are wrong, we could end up in hell. Therefore, Pascal regarded it as sensible for us to assume that God does exist and live accordingly, because that way we can only win. We cannot lose.

> ★ Do not make generalisations about any religion or religious group. Statements like 'Christians believe the world was created in seven days' are inaccurate and will weaken your arguments.

Imagination

Some people are reluctant to consider imagination as a way of knowing, particularly in the area of religious knowledge. They may be concerned with the historicity of religious narratives and believe that unless narratives are historically accurate, they are fictional and therefore 'untrue'. Others would argue that narratives can convey profound truths whether the narratives are historically true or not.

In many religious traditions, imagination has played a significant role in discovering, articulating and transmitting religious knowledge. **Parables** and fables are simple short stories that illustrate moral teachings, and can be found in a number of religious traditions. Imaginative **myths** have also been used to explain the world, relationships and rituals and to teach different ideologies, morals and behavioural models.

> **parable**: a short story that conveys a truth or moral ideal
>
> **myth**: a traditional story about gods, heroes or groups of people

Faith

Mark Twain famously wrote 'Faith is believing something you know ain't true.' But faith is not as far distant from reason as Twain's comment might lead us to believe.

The word 'faith' comes from the Latin *fidere*, which means to trust, and a great deal of religious knowledge is accepted on trust. But it is not necessarily a trust without evidence, or a trust that flies in the face of evidence; it is a trust and

> ℹ Although some myths may be based on actual events and people, the word 'myth' is sometimes used in casual language to mean a lie or an untrue story. It is perhaps not surprising, therefore, that in many religions there is considerable disagreement among believers about which narratives, if any, are mythical.

"Faith means believing in things you've never seen...like your feet!"

confidence in something for which we have enough evidence to justify our belief though not enough for incontrovertible proof.

Although the words *religion* and *faith* are often used interchangeably, faith is not limited to religion. In many areas of life we develop theories and conclusions based on our experiences. This is inductive reasoning which we considered in Chapter 6.

When I set my alarm clock for 6 a.m., my alarm always goes off at 6 a.m. Each time I set it, I take it on trust that it will work based on my experience that it has worked in the past. I cannot prove in advance that it will work tomorrow morning, but I believe that it will work, even though it is always possible, and indeed probable, that there will come a morning when it will not work.

A great deal of the knowledge we rely on in our day-to-day lives is necessarily grounded in faith. That faith is based on the evidence of our experiences and is not diminished by the lack of concrete proof. In determining whether or not to have faith, we must employ other ways of knowing including our sensory perceptions, emotions, intuition, memory, imagination and reason.

Do not make generalisations about ways of knowing. Statements like 'Religious knowledge depends on imagination and faith while science relies on perception and reason' are inaccurate and misleading.

Task: think about

- Does science rely on faith as much as religion does? What about history?
- 'Where there is doubt, there must always be faith.' To what extent do you think this is true?
- How does faith differ from belief?
- To what extent is faith based on our own experiences the same as faith based upon reports of the experiences of others from long ago?

Real-life situation

In January 2006 the name *Allah* as written in Arabic was recognised in the pattern of spots along one side of a two-year-old albino Oscar (a species of fish). On the other side of the fish was the name *Muhammad*. Within hours of the discovery, the fish was at the centre of a media frenzy, and people flocked to the pet shop where the fish resided. Many people declared the markings on the fish to be a miracle and that the fish was a sign from Allah. Others saw it as just a pretty fish.

- What might justify people interpreting the markings on the fish as names?
- What might justify people claiming the markings to be a miracle?
- On the basis of the account given, are you inclined to believe the fish to be a sign from Allah or to be sceptical? What evidence would you need to persuade you to change your view?

Choose a real-life situation from your own experience that has made you think: something from your own religious tradition or a personal encounter with another tradition.

Can you discern Arabic writing on the side of this fish?

Knowledge questions

- What kinds of assumptions do we make when we attempt to interpret patterns in different areas of knowledge?
- To what extent do different kinds of truth require different ways of knowing?

Presentation task

Think about a real-life situation related to religion. What are some general questions the situation raises? Try to develop a knowledge question that arises from the situation. You may want to plan a presentation based on your knowledge question.

Extended writing task

Write 500 words on one or more of the following questions:

1 What roles might the different ways of knowing play in determining whether a miracle has occurred?

2 How might the number of people making a knowledge claim affect our willingness to accept the truth of the claim?

3 To what extent can we rely on the opinion of authorities when assessing a claim for knowledge?

Prescribed essay titles

1 'All knowledge claims should be open to rational criticism.' On what grounds and to what extent would you agree with this assertion? (November 2009 and May 2010)

2 Belief has been described as 'certainty about what cannot be seen'. Does this statement hold true in any, some or all areas of knowledge? (November 2006 and May 2007)

3 'People need to believe that order can be glimpsed in the chaos of events' (adapted from John Gray, *Heresies,* 2004). In what ways and to what extent would you say this claim is relevant in at least two areas of knowledge? (November 2009 and May 2010)

Further reading and sources

Armstrong, Karen. 2009. *The Case for God.* The Bodley Head.

Lewis, Paul. *'A fish called Allah',* The Guardian, 2 February 2006.
   Available at: www.guardian.co.uk/uk/2006/feb/02/paullewis

Princeton University, *'Anselm's ontological argument'.*
   Available at: www.princeton.edu/~grosen/puc/phi203/ontological.html

Smart, Ninian. 1991. *The Religious Experience.* Macmillan.

12 Indigenous knowledge framework

Introduction

Indigenous peoples are distinct communities whose identities and customs are inextricably linked to a land they have inhabited for many generations. Depending on the definitions adopted, there are estimated to be 270–370 million indigenous people in the world living in 70 countries.

Indigenous people are usually self-identified as indigenous and they claim continuity with pre-colonial communities as well as strong links to the land in which they live. Typically they have their own distinct languages, as well as distinct political and social systems. Embodied in their lifestyles, beliefs and traditions is a body of indigenous knowledge that has accumulated over decades or even centuries of living in a particular environment.

Over generations, many indigenous peoples have intermarried with immigrants and neighbouring peoples. This often raises significant debates about who the indigenous peoples are. Different countries have resolved the problem in different ways.

The New Zealand government, for example, defines a Maori as 'a person of the

Because of high rates of intermarriage, there are very few if any 'pure' Maori today. However, under New Zealand law anyone with a Maori ancestor can claim indigenous rights.

Maori race of New Zealand; and includes any descendant of such a person'. In this case, any person with just one Maori ancestor, however remote, may claim indigenous rights as a Maori. In Australia, the Australian High Court defined an Aboriginal or Torres Strait Islander as 'a person of Aboriginal or Torres Strait Islander descent who identifies as an Aboriginal or Torres Strait Islander and is accepted as such by the community in which he or she lives'. Other countries such as Canada have adopted more legalistic definitions, which may depend upon factors relating to parentage and marriage.

In practice it is often people who live rurally who continue to identify with their indigenous roots. Those in cities tend to be assimilated into a broader culture, particularly if they intermarry. Many of their indigenous skills and knowledge are no longer necessary in urban living and are often lost. But this is not always the case; there are some city dwellers who still strongly identify with their indigenous origins.

Task: think about

- Where does an indigenous culture stop and more general society begin? Why does it matter?
- If we have our own strong cultural traditions how are we different from indigenous peoples?
- How many generations should there be in a particular place for a population to be regarded as indigenous?
- If members of a recognised indigenous group such as the Izhorians of Russia move from their recognised homeland to a multicultural city, for how many generations could we regard their descendants as being indigenous Izhorians?
- If all people originated in the Rift Valley in Africa, to what extent are any of us indigenous to other places?

Task: activity

Investigate the histories of indigenous peoples in your own country, and if you doubt whether there are any, discover when identifiably indigenous peoples were last there and why they died out, if indeed they have.

What is indigenous knowledge?

Indigenous knowledge is knowledge that is predominantly related to community survival in a particular environment. It often involves a deep understanding of local ecology, and includes beliefs and practices that are embedded in the community's culture. This knowledge can sometimes be used to maintain social, economic and ecological sustainability for indigenous communities.

In recent years there has been a growing appreciation of the valuable contributions indigenous knowledge can make to the rest of the world in fields as diverse as conservation, agriculture and medical science. For example, the rosy periwinkle is a plant native to Madagascar, and natives used it as a medicinal plant. Researchers were able to derive the drug vinblastine from it, and this drug is now used to treat Hodgkin's lymphoma.

Indigenous peoples are sometimes believed to have a deep or even innate understanding of how much can be harvested from the land, how many animals can be killed, and how to balance hunger and need with husbandry and stewardship if they are to have anything to eat next year or in future generations.

ⓘ Indigenous knowledge is not necessarily restricted to indigenous peoples. It can occur wherever a group of people have lived off the land or in a particular environment for generations, whether they are indigenous or not.

innate knowledge: the knowledge we are born with

It is a debatable issue as to whether there is such a thing as **innate knowledge**. Some people believe we have no knowledge when we are born and that all our knowledge comes from experience; others argue that some of our knowledge is innate. Several contemporary philosophers have entered the debate, including Stephen Pinker and Noam Chomsky.

Task: think about

- Why do you think there has been a growing interest in indigenous knowledge in the twentieth and twenty-first centuries?
- To what extent could ignorance of indigenous knowledge lie at the heart of the current global ecological crisis?
- Could there be such a thing as global indigenous knowledge over the preservation and stewardship of the Earth's resources?

Real–life situation

The Bhotia men of Uttar Pradesh, India, traditionally herded sheep and grew cotton while the women wove carpets from the wool tied with home-grown cotton. In recent decades synthetic materials and chemical dyes have replaced the natural materials, but the chemical dyes are carcinogenic and pollute the environment.

There is now a programme underway to revive traditional carpet-weaving in the Kumaon region, drawing upon the Bhotia people's indigenous knowledge of carpet-weaving, sheep-farming and cotton-growing. This programme is driven, in part, by the high demand for non-synthetic carpets in Europe, where natural carpets retail for three times the price of synthetic carpets.

Be careful not to over-generalise. All indigenous peoples are not the same. Each group is unique, with its own ways of living, beliefs and customs. If you are writing about indigenous knowledge, use specific examples. You should also take care not to romanticise indigenous cultures; they can be just as unjust, destructive and imperfect as any other culture.

A Bhotian woman making a traditional rug. Is the revival of such skills beneficial to indigenous people or does it exploit them?

Task: think about

The growing respect for indigenous knowledge by people outside the indigenous group is, in part, due to the recognition of the usefulness of that knowledge to outsiders.

- To what extent do you think the revival of indigenous knowledge in Uttar Pradesh is driven by a concern for health and the environment and to what extent is it driven by the desire for greater profits? Does it matter?
- How might a growing demand for natural carpets have a detrimental effect on the Kumaon environment? Does it matter?
- Does encouraging the local people of Kumaon to continue their traditional practices limit their options for progress or restrict their development? Does it matter, and to whom?
- To what extent might the indigenous knowledge of the Bhotia people be transferable to other communities? What might be the consequences for the Bhotia people if it is transferable?

Where does indigenous knowledge come from?

We have seen what indigenous knowledge is, but where does it come from? How do indigenous peoples come to know what they know?

Indigenous language

Language is a primary means of knowledge transmission for humans, and indigenous languages often express ideas or concepts for which there are no equivalent words in other languages. Therefore indigenous language is an essential means of transmission for indigenous knowledge.

It is estimated that 95% of the world's 6800 languages are spoken by no more than 5% of the world's population. Some of these languages have fewer than 1000 speakers and many of them are unwritten because they have no formal script. In such languages, indigenous knowledge is passed orally from one generation to the next without being codified in writing or translated into any languages with wider access. This means that if the indigenous language is lost, the indigenous knowledge will be lost with it.

Kyung-wha Kang, the UN Deputy High Commissioner for Human Rights, claims that 43% of the world's languages are in danger of extinction. Preserving indigenous languages has become a priority for many people who wish to preserve indigenous knowledge.

Compare the key concepts and language of indigenous knowledge with other areas of knowledge. Think about the following:

- In indigenous knowledge tribal languages often embody concepts that do not translate well. In what way is this issue similar to or different from language issues in other areas of knowledge?

Task: think about

- To what extent would introducing writing systems to people with unwritten languages help to preserve indigenous knowledge?
- Could indigenous languages be translated into widely used languages such as English, Arabic, Mandarin or Hindi? To what extent might translation alter the knowledge conveyed by indigenous languages?
- If indigenous languages were to be translated, would the indigenous knowledge they convey be more widely accessible?

Praxis

Many skills are passed on from one generation to the next through an apprenticeship-like system in which, typically, fathers teach their sons, and mothers teach their daughters. Among the Aboriginal people of Australia, girls are taken aside when they reach puberty to be taught 'women's business' by the womenfolk. This includes teaching them the knowledge and skills deemed necessary to prepare them for marriage and motherhood. Similarly, when the boys reach puberty, the men of their ethnic group put them through a series of initiation rites to prepare them for manhood. Women are not allowed to be party to these initiation rites, just as men are not allowed to know the secrets that are passed on to the girls.

The skills that are passed on in any indigenous society may involve hunting, cooking, farming, craftsmanship, bushmanship, knowledge of where to find or how to grow good pasture, where to find and access safe water, and how to develop natural medicines, and so on. These are skills which can only fully be learnt through practising them. For example, although most of us could read and follow a recipe in a cookery book, the best cooks learn through years of cooking alongside experts, whether within the family or with professional chefs. (This is why many people think professional cooking, like many careers, is best learnt through an apprenticeship system.)

Sensory perceptions form an integral part of **praxis**. In learning to cook we need to rely on our senses of smell and taste to be certain we have added the right ingredients in the right quantities and followed the right procedures, and we need the guidance of experience. For many indigenous people, even knowing what can be eaten and in what quantities at what times of the year is a matter of life and death, and all such knowledge must be handed down from generation to generation.

Just as we can read a cookery book, so we could read a book about hunting. But to be a skilled hunter (whether with a gun, a spear or a camera) a person needs to hunt with experts to develop the skills necessary to read animal tracks, interpret the sounds of the jungle, scrubland or prairies and anticipate where the prey may be found.

Practising a skill allows our body to get a sense of what is right. If we listen to birds in the forest with an expert, our ears will gradually become attuned to the different sounds birds make and we will begin to develop the discerning skills of the expert.

praxis: the established practice or custom of any group

Gamelan music players. Children learn traditional skills by practising them alongside their elders.

Task: think about

- Could you become a good footballer or musician by reading every 'how to' book ever written but never actually playing?
- Which skills can we learn from manuals and which must we learn through praxis?
- What are the advantages and disadvantages of each method of learning?

Authority

It is common in many indigenous cultures for authorities such as elders, chieftains or shamans to act as guardians of indigenous knowledge. These authorities may be appointed or elected, or attain their position through inheritance. The indigenous knowledge they preserve may relate to areas as diverse as religious beliefs and practices, environmental knowledge, tribal history, tribal laws and indigenous crafts and skills. Authority figures are frequently responsible for decision-making, maintaining indigenous traditions and upholding cultural norms within their communities. They may be considered guardians of the collective memory.

In some cases the authorities within an ethnic group will forbid their knowledge to be shared outside the group. Elders of some Native American ethnic groups, for example, fear exploitation and will disown any member of the group who shares their knowledge of tribal medicines with outsiders.

Task: think about

- Without documentary evidence, how can we be sure that tribal authorities transmit indigenous knowledge accurately?
- Could the ways in which authorities are appointed affect the reliability of the knowledge that is preserved?
- To what extent can respect for indigenous knowledge lead to the exploitation of it?
- Do you think the sharing of indigenous knowledge can damage it in some way?

Faith

As we have already seen, faith is an important way of knowing in many knowledge areas. Faith is also important for indigenous knowledge, particularly when related to culture and traditions. People need to have faith in their stories and traditions in order to preserve them. When people lose faith in their beliefs, the beliefs, and the practices associated with them, are lost.

There is a strong connection between traditional medicines and belief systems in many indigenous cultures. The Bantu people who live in Zimbabwe, for example, have a holistic system of traditional medicine which considers illnesses in terms of physical, emotional, psychological, spiritual and environmental imbalances. Bantu healers often consult the spirit world to reach their diagnoses, and their medical practices are inseparable from traditional Bantu religion. It is claimed that the use of traditional medicines requires significant faith in both the spirit world and the ability of the healer to act as a medium.

Task: think about

- Why would faith in spirits be necessary for physical healing in Bantu culture?
- Is knowledge that is accepted by faith alone really knowledge?

Compare the links to personal knowledge in the indigenous knowledge systems with other areas of knowledge. Think about the following:

- How might indigenous knowledge systems expand your insights or deepen your awareness of yourself, others or the society and world in which you live?
- How do individuals make a contribution to our shared knowledge in indigenous knowledge systems?

Indigenous knowledge is not static. As with all knowledge, it develops and changes over time. As indigenous peoples undergo different experiences, are exposed to changes in their environment, and meet with people of different cultures, so their ideas, beliefs and practices change.

Imagination

Imagination can be a powerful way of gaining indigenous knowledge. Storytelling is an important vehicle for the transmission of knowledge for many indigenous peoples, particularly those without a written language system. Indeed, an oral tradition was the norm in all cultures before printed materials became widely available, and many of our most ancient texts are themselves records of stories and events that had been passed down orally for generations before.

People of all cultures create stories to help teach their children. For indigenous peoples, stories are an effective way of teaching future generations knowledge that is essential to survival as well as knowledge deemed valuable to their culture.

The Dreamtime stories of Australian Aborigines are a clear example of this. Many of the Dreamtime stories are about animals and people that can be seen as patterns in the stars of the night sky. These stories help people to remember and recognise certain stars. This knowledge then enables them to use these stars to navigate across the vast Australian bush and deserts. Accurate navigation is as essential to survival in the Australian outback as it is at sea.

As well as passing on knowledge useful for navigation, the Dreamtime stories also include important information about animal behaviour and habitats. This knowledge can be vital for survival for people who live off the land.

If you live in a large town or city, you may find it difficult to understand how people can see animals and people in the patterns made by stars, because you probably do not get to see many stars in the night sky. But in the Australian outback there is virtually no light pollution and often no cloud cover, so you can see thousands of stars lighting up the sky. It is a magical sight.

Compare the methodology used to gain indigenous knowledge with methodologies used other areas of knowledge. Think about the following:

- Praxis is an important means of transmitting indigenous knowledge. How does this compare with knowledge transmission in other areas of knowledge?

Can you see any animals in this night sky?

> **Task: think about**
>
> - Why might stories make it easier to learn and remember important information?
> - To what extent is indigenous knowledge dependent upon imagination?
> - To what extent do you think the landscape and sky are more meaningful for indigenous peoples?
> - To what extent do you think the landscape and sky are more meaningful for rural people, whether indigenous or not?

Intuition

Whether intuition is a sense in itself or whether it is a subconscious reading of subtle signs is a debatable issue. Either way, it can be an important way of knowing for indigenous people. Intuition can play a part in helping people to decide what crops to plant, where to hunt or fish, and where to find water. These decisions can be essential for the survival and well-being of an ethnic group, particularly those who live in inhospitable terrains.

One example can be drawn from the Subay people, a Bedouin group of Saudi Arabia. The genuinely nomadic life of Bedouin is fast disappearing and most Subay people are now settled in cities, but a few still live in their traditional way. These nomadic Subay people are very adept at finding water and pasture for their livestock. Some would say that this ability is intuitive, and that their intuition enables them to know where to find fresh water and pasture in the desert.

> **Task: think about**
>
> - What, if anything, do you know intuitively?
> - To what extent must we all rely on our intuition?
> - If intuition does involve unconscious reading of signs, how might the skill be passed from one generation to another through living together in a community?

Reason

A great deal of indigenous knowledge is discovered through reason. In many cases this will be the result of inductive reasoning through regular and repeated observations of the local environment. For example, people may observe over the years that some local plants are more resistant to drought than others, or they may observe that animal behaviours differ under different weather conditions. Over time, these observations become regarded as truths, which help the holders of these truths to survive and prosper.

The local knowledge accumulated by indigenous peoples may not only be of local value; sometimes the knowledge they acquire has universal applications. For example, the Quechua people of Bolivia and Peru discovered the bark of the cinchona tree could be used to reduce fever and inflammation. When scientific studies were conducted it was discovered that the tree bark produces a chemical we now know as quinine. Quinine became the first effective treatment for malaria and has been used around the world.

Compare the scope and applications of indigenous knowledge with other areas of knowledge. Think about the following:

- Indigenous knowledge is often localised and may be based on beliefs and practices that are difficult to understand in other contexts. How does this compare with other areas of knowledge?

There are many 'alternative' health care systems around the world, some of which are based on indigenous knowledge. These include ayurvedic medicine in India and Sri Lanka, acupuncture in China, and Native American medicines in North America.

- To what extent should these medical practices be subjected to scientific testing?
- To what extent should they be expected to meet modern (western) medical standards?
- The British actor and comedian Stephen Fry has suggested that if alternative medicines worked, they would simply be known as 'medicine'. To what extent do you agree with him?
- If the failure of a local health cure is attributed to the lack of faith of the recipient, is this a reasonable defence?
- To what extent does such a defence immunise the practice from criticism?

Real-life situation

In Madagascar, the position of Tompondrano (keeper of the lakes) is a lifelong position that is traditionally passed down to the first son when the existing Tompondrano dies. The position of Tompondrano is an important one because it is the Tompondrano who makes significant decisions concerning the lakes, such as when the fishing season can begin.

When the last Tompondrano of the Soamalipo and Befotaka Lakes died, it is said that his second son wanted to be the Tompondrano and so he deceived the villagers into thinking his older brother had deserted the community. With his older brother away, the second son then claimed the title for himself. An inauguration ceremony was held in which the second son was instated. Once in post he could not be removed, even when his older brother returned, thus he gained the coveted position by deception. That year the fishing in the lakes was poor and villagers believed the ancestors had deliberately withheld the fish because they were upset by the new Tompondrano's behaviour.

- Is the villagers' explanation for the poor fishing that year reasonable?
- To what extent does your answer depend on your willingness to believe that the ancestors of the villagers have the power to affect the fishing?
- Can the nature of what is reasonable be determined by cultural context?
- How does your society explain unusual environmental events?
- To what extent might you regard indigenous knowledge systems as more holistic than your own cultural knowledge systems?

Could angry ancestors be responsible for poor fishing?

Knowledge questions

- To what extent can there be reasons that make sense locally without faith in the underlying cultural principles?
- To what extent can there be faith in local practices without reasons to believe in them?

Presentation task

Think about a real-life situation in which local knowledge has played a significant role. What are some general questions that the situation raises? Try to develop a knowledge question that arises from the situation.

Extended writing task

Write 500 words on one or more of the following questions:

1 To what extent can indigenous knowledge be applied to situations outside the environment in which the people who develop that knowledge live?

2 How might we evaluate a knowledge claim that is based on indigenous knowledge?

3 With reference to at least two ways of knowing, explain the difference between superstition and indigenous knowledge.

Prescribed essay topics

1 Does language play roles of equal importance in different areas of knowledge? (November 2007 and May 2008)

2 Evaluate the strengths and weaknesses of reason as a way of knowing. (November 2008 and May 2009)

3 How can the different ways of knowing help us to distinguish between something that is true and something that is believed to be true?
(November 2009 and May 2010)

Further reading and sources

Australian Law Reform Commission, *'Kinship and identity: Legal definitions of Aboriginality.'*
  Available at: www.alrc.gov.au/publications/36-kinship-and-identity/legal-definitions-aboriginality
Kazembe, Takawira. 2007. *'Traditional medicine in Zimbabwe.'* Rose Croix Journal.
  Available at: www.rosecroixjournal.org/issues/2007/articles/vol4_55_72_kazembe.pdf
McKay, Helen. *'The Dreamtime – Australian Aboriginal storytelling.'* Bushcraft and Survival 16 June 2010.
  Available at: http://bushcraftandsurvival.blogspot.in/2010/06/dreamtime-australian-aboriginal.html
Norrell, Brenda. *'UN Human Rights Council: Preserving indigenous languages.'* The Narcosphere. 20 September
  2011. Available at: http://narcosphere.narconews.com/notebook/brenda-norrell/2011/09/un-human-rights-
  council-preserving-indigenous-languages
Statistics New Zealand, *'Maori descent: definition.'* Available at: www.stats.govt.nz/surveys_and_methods/methods/
  classifications-andstandards/classification-related-stats-standards/maori-descent/definition.aspx
Tingay, Ruth. *'Notes from the field: July 2000 (Part 2)',* The Peregrine Fund in Madagascar Project. 14 July 2000.
  Available at: http://blogs.peregrinefund.org/article/340
UNESCO, *'Languages and writing.'* Available at: http://portal.unesco.org/education/en/ev.php-URL_ID=28301&URL_
  DO=DO_TOPIC&URL_SECTION=201.html

13 Understanding the assessment requirements

Introduction

The essay is an enquiry or investigation into a knowledge question. It involves an analysis of the question and the connections and links between particular areas of knowledge and ways of knowing.

Towards the end of your TOK course you will write an essay which will be externally assessed by the IB. The examiner will award a mark based on the holistic marking scheme. There are two overall holistic features that are used to judge the merits of a TOK essay: *understanding* knowledge questions and *analysing* knowledge questions. Chapters 13–16 aim to explain the assessment criteria and outline some of the features of an excellent TOK essay. There is no prescribed content for a TOK essay and what you write has to be entirely your decision. Your essay is uniquely yours and needs to reflect your own critical thinking. It needs to answer the question, focus on knowledge, and explore links and comparisons between areas of knowledge and ways of knowing. This chapter offers some advice which you can use at your discretion, but there are no prescribed formulae for a successful essay.

IB assessment

The essay is externally assessed by an IB examiner using holistic / global impression marking. It is uploaded electronically and e-marked; see the *Handbook of Procedures for the Diploma Programme* which teachers can find on the IB Online Curriculum Centre (OCC) website.

In each examination session the International Baccalaureate (IB) publishes TOK prescribed titles (PTs) for the essay. There are six essay titles from which to choose. You choose one from the list and answer it in no more than 1600 words. If you are taking your IB examinations in May, the titles are published in the previous September. For the November session, the titles are available from March. Your teacher can find them on the IB Online Curriculum Centre (OCC) website.

There are 10 marks awarded for the essay. Your essay mark is worth 67% of your final TOK score; your presentation mark makes up the remaining 33% of the marks. The essay is submitted electronically and externally assessed by IB examiners using e-marking.

Examples of prescribed essay titles can be found at the end of each chapter in Units 1 and 2. A TOK essay is *an investigation or enquiry* into a knowledge question. It is not a research essay, like your Extended Essay. Knowledge questions are open-ended, comparative, about knowledge or knowing, expressed in TOK vocabulary and they lend themselves to thoughtful enquiry.

As explained in Units 1 and 2, there are eight **areas of knowledge**: mathematics, science, human science, history, the arts, ethics, religious knowledge systems and indigenous knowledge systems. There are also eight **ways of knowing**: emotion, reason, memory, faith, language, imagination, intuition and sense perception. TOK essays are about knowledge and they invite you to make *links and comparisons* between areas of knowledge and ways of knowing. An essay title requires you to show your skills of analysis by making these connections.

Essays test your ability to think critically about knowledge. In your essay you will show analytical skills by:

- evaluating arguments, knowledge claims and counter-claims
- weighing up evidence
- identifying assumptions and implications.

Think of your essay as a *branching essay*, which considers a range of possible views. Your task is to shape an intelligent response to a knowledge question. TOK essays are never about subject-specific questions, such as 'How do we know if different interpretations of the Cold War were justified?' Instead knowledge questions go beyond subject-specific concerns and focus on knowledge questions, for example: 'How do we know if theories lead to reliable knowledge in history and science?'

The point of an essay is to bring critical thought to the title. You should aim to write in clear and precise language. However, students who are writing their essay in their second or third language will not lose marks for a minor lack of fluency, unless it becomes a significant problem for understanding the text. It is reassuring to know that your essay is not a language test. Equally, fluently written essays are not good essays if they do not address knowledge questions or include a strong level of analysis.

Holistic marking is also known as global impression marking and is based on the overall quality of your essay. Your essay will be awarded one of five levels of achievement, depending on its quality, with 5 being the highest level and 0 the lowest. There are descriptions for each level published by the IB.

The following table is based on information given in the IB subject guide.

Level 5 (top level)	9–10 marks (maximum marks)
Level 4	7–8 marks
Level 3	5–6 marks
Level 2	3–4 marks
Level 1	1–2 marks
	0 marks

- Answer the exact title prescribed and do not change the wording in any way.
- Do not write more than the word limit of 1600 words. Examiners are asked to stop reading beyond this and deduct 1 mark. State your total number of words when you upload your essay.

Does the student present an appropriate and cogent analysis of knowledge questions in discussing the title?

Has the student:

- understood the proposition?
- understood the knowledge questions that are explicit and implicit in the title, and/or linked the proposition to knowledge questions?
- developed a comprehensive and cogent point of view about the topic and appropriate knowledge questions?

The holistic judgement of your essay is based around this main question.

Task: activity

Think of your essay title in relation to other aspects of TOK thinking. Make notes on:

a the connections between the prescribed essay title and parts of the knowledge framework

b the connections and links with knowledge questions, ways of knowing, areas of knowledge, personal and shared knowledge and any examples that support your analysis of the question.

An IB examiners' report is published after every examination session. It comments on candidates' work and offers advice for future candidates. It is worth reading this advice. Exemplar TOK essays with examiners' comments explain the marks awarded to particular essays. Your teacher can find these and various other resources and documents on the IB Online Curriculum Centre: http://occ.ibo.org

Other resources can be bought from the IB store: http://store.ibo.org

It's an important skill to identify relevant knowledge questions in relation to an essay title. You should also be able to spot knowledge questions which are not relevant to an essay title.

Understanding and analysing knowledge questions

The examiner will make an overall judgement about your essay based on two features: your *understanding* of knowledge questions and your *analysis* of knowledge questions (see table below). If your essay is focused on showing your understanding of knowledge questions and an intelligent analysis of them, it should be developing along the right lines.

Understanding knowledge questions	Analysis of knowledge questions
• connections with knowledge questions • relevant knowledge questions • depth and breadth • links and comparisons • connections with ways of knowing • connections with areas of knowledge • investigation of alternative perspectives	• enquiry • sound justification • clear and coherent argument • real-life examples • extensive exploration of counter-claims • assumptions identified • implications considered • evaluation

Remember that there is no rigid list of features necessary to achieve each level. Examiners will look at your essay individually and judge your overall performance. The IB gives descriptions of each level of performance and it is worth looking carefully at these descriptions (see page 127) with your teacher so that you understand them.

Your essay is a response to one prescribed title. The relevant knowledge question is clearly the title itself. There may be directly related knowledge questions that arise from the title that you could also address. For the title 'To what extent do theories lead to certain knowledge in ethics and science?' you might also consider 'To what extent do the **methods** used in science and ethics provide us with certain knowledge?' and 'To what extent are **theories** similar in ethics and science?' These 'subsidiary' knowledge questions may be important in relation to the main title. Take care to identify relevant knowledge questions. You don't want to go off on a tangent, fail to answer the main title itself or identify irrelevant knowledge questions. Make sure that any knowledge questions you identify are always relevant to answering the prescribed essay title.

Depth and breadth

The balance of breadth and depth varies between essay titles, but, whichever essay title you choose, your writing needs to demonstrate *both* types of thinking, depth and breadth of thought, to demonstrate your awareness of connections.

By depth of understanding is meant detailed knowledge within an area of knowledge or way of knowing. A deep understanding of history might involve making a distinction between historical facts and historical interpretations. In the arts you might distinguish between the types of knowledge that the different art forms offer. With ways of knowing, a deep understanding of the role of reason might involve making a distinction between reason and rationality, or inductive and deductive reasoning. Understanding the role of memory might involve a distinction between working memory, long-term memory and autobiographical memory.

Breadth is about thinking of connections, links and comparisons. If you choose a title that focuses on just history, you are expected to show your awareness of the breadth of connections with ways of knowing.

Knowledge can mean different things in different contexts, and each area of knowledge has its unique method. A historian's imagination needs to be consistent with an interpretation of primary and secondary sources, whereas artists can use their imagination freely, but art forms may need to conform to some conventional standards. By comparing our knowledge in history and the arts, we might draw out the different meanings of 'knowledge'. Facts in history might include dates that can be checked against the evidence, whereas a fact in the arts could include the form of music or poetry or a fact about the historical context of literature. Your essay will explore the distinctions, links and comparisons between areas of knowledge and ways of knowing and use real-life examples to illustrate your points.

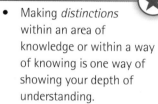

Think about the connections between personal and shared knowledge in different subject areas.

- Making *distinctions* within an area of knowledge or within a way of knowing is one way of showing your depth of understanding.
- Make distinctions when you use the word 'knowledge'. Consider what we mean by knowledge in different contexts.

Task: activity

1 Identify any relevant knowledge questions for one of these IB prescribed essay titles:

   a Discuss the claim that some areas of knowledge are discovered and others are invented. (November 2009 and May 2010)

   b How important are the opinions of experts in the search for knowledge? (November 2010 and May 2011)

   c To what extent do we need evidence to support our beliefs in different areas of knowledge? (November 2010 and May 2011)

2 Consider the following list of *distinctions*. Think of ways in which you might apply some of these distinctions to the essay titles above.

- personal and shared knowledge
- fact and interpretation
- **hypothesis** and **conjecture**
- finite and infinite
- justified reasoning and **fallacious reasoning**
- 'knowing that' and 'knowing how'
- intellectual and practical knowledge
- nature and culture

3 Consider how you might include your own distinctions to demonstrate your depth of understanding in your essay.

hypothesis: a possible explanation or prediction used as a starting point for investigation

conjecture: a claim based on a speculation or guesswork

fallacious reasoning: reasoning based on errors or mistakes

Summary

Key features of the essay

What the essay is	What the essay is not
an enquiry or investigation into a knowledge question	a research essay like the Extended Essay
knowledge-specific	subject-specific
about knowledge and knowing	about subject-specific information
an analysis of the connections and links between areas of knowledge and ways of knowing	a plain description of areas of knowledge or ways of knowing

Assessment

Who assesses the essay?	Externally assessed by an IB examiner using e-marking
What is the word limit?	1600 words
How is the essay marked?	Holistic / global impression marking
How much it is worth?	67% of the total marks for TOK
What is the maximum score?	10 marks
How many essay titles are there to choose from?	Answer one from a choice of six prescribed titles
How is the essay submitted?	It is uploaded electronically; see the 'Handbook of Procedures for the Diploma Programme' which teachers can find on the OCC website

14 Analysis, links and comparisons

Introduction

In this chapter we offer some clear tools and methods for analysis, an important feature of a good essay. The whole purpose of TOK is critical thinking, and your essay needs to demonstrate good analysis of a knowledge question.

Prescribed essay titles lend themselves to analysis rather than description. Whereas a descriptive essay might give an account, an analytical essay would bring some critical thought to bear on the topic. Good analysis would involve weighing up evidence behind the different positions taken, and assessing the relative merits of each to reach a balanced judgement. Unlike description, analysis demonstrates your own critical thought, consideration and intelligent judgement. A good analytical essay, unlike a descriptive essay, demonstrates **higher-order thinking skills**.

The diagram shown here is a useful way of highlighting the distinction between description and analysis. Below the line represents critical thinking, TOK concepts and TOK tools for analysis. Above the line represents your IB subjects, specific areas of knowledge, real-life situations and your own examples. Your essay title and other knowledge questions connected to it are from below the line. Your essay begins below the line and you can briefly describe subject specific examples from above the line (say science experiments, or books you've studied) and relate them back to the TOK questions, ideas and concepts from below the line. Your essay connects knowledge questions and TOK thinking to the ordinary world. (Your presentation works in the opposite direction, beginning with a description of a real-life example from above the line and extracting and analysing a knowledge question from below the line.)

Analysis of knowledge questions will gain you marks under the holistic marking scheme in your assessed essay. Essays that take a descriptive approach often gain poor marks.

> **higher-order thinking skills** (according to Bloom's Taxonomy) include: evaluation, synthesis, analysis, application, comprehension and knowledge

Real-life situation
Vocabulary specific to area of knowledge
Knowledge questions
General TOK vocabulary

Below the line represents TOK: critical thinking, TOK concepts and TOK tools for analysis. Above the line represents subject-specific areas of knowledge and real-life situations.

For homework, a class has been asked to plan an essay based on an IB prescribed title 'Are reason and emotion equally necessary in justifying moral decisions?' (November 2007 and May 2008).

Having discussed the title in class, the students come up with a plan. Bethan is planning to write her essay with plenty of descriptive examples to illustrate how we use both reason and emotion when making moral decisions. She wants to gather many examples from different areas of knowledge. Tom is taking a theoretical approach with lots of philosophical references to key thinkers. Paulo is planning an analytical essay looking at different positions he could take on the question, exploring the various 'sides' to the question and making use of personal examples based on what he has learnt in his IB subjects.

- Compare the different approaches to the question. What advice would you give to each student about their plan?

Unpacking knowledge questions

Studying the question closely: language and key terms

When you choose your title, think carefully about the wording of the question and make sure that you understand what the title means. It's important that you know what the essay requires, and decoding the **command words** and **key concepts** in the title (in this case, truth, but it could be 'explanation' or 'evidence') will give you a strong clue. The following question was set as a prescribed title in November 2009 and May 2010: 'To what extent is the truth different in mathematics, the arts and ethics?' Here the key TOK concept is 'truth' and the command words are 'to what extent'.

The title requires you to form a judgement about the relative extent to which the concept of truth is different in the three areas of knowledge. Other command words might include *evaluate, consider, how important, on what grounds, discuss* or *examine*. Take time to understand the meaning of the words in the context of the essay question. The command words need to be understood in relation to the particular question; the following list explains each one.

command words: instructions that tell you what to do in the essay; for example, 'to what extent' or 'on what grounds'

key concept: some essays have a central idea to explore such as the concept of 'explanation' or the idea of 'certainty'

Definitions of some command words

Evaluate	Weigh up and form a judgement
Consider	Think critically about, give critical thought to
How important	Form a judgement about relative importance (very important? not that important?)
On what grounds	Consider what the criteria would be or reasons
To what extent	Evaluate and form a judgement about the relative extent (to a large extent? to a limited extent?) supported by sound argument
Discuss	Look at both sides and come up with your own answer
Examine	Look at and consider critically

When you choose your essay title, play to your strengths. Consider what you have enjoyed about the course and which title you have something to say about. If you are inspired to write it, you are likely to write an engaging essay. On the other hand if you feel very strongly about a title be careful that you do not write a one-sided essay with a closed perspective and no consideration of alternative views. Whichever title you choose, you need to be able to interpret the title in an open-minded way as you will need to consider it from different perspectives. If you only have one point with lots of examples to back it up that will lead to an essay that is repeating just one idea.

The emphasis of titles varies. Look carefully at the language used in the title and make sure you understand the important terms. Some focus explicitly on one area of knowledge, for example science or history. Other titles might focus on one particular way of knowing, for example reason, imagination or another key concept (such as truth, evidence or methodology).

> **Task: activity**
>
> 1 For each of the essay titles below, identify the command words and key concepts.
> 2 Identify the relevant knowledge questions raised by one or more of the titles.
>   a Discuss the roles of language and reason in history. (November 2010 and May 2011)
>   b 'There are no absolute distinctions between what is true and what is false'. Discuss this claim. (November 2010 and May 2011)
>   c Examine the ways empirical evidence should be used to make progress in different areas of knowledge. (November 2009 and May 2010)

Aspect	Level 5 Excellent 9–10	Level 4 Very good 7–8
Understanding knowledge questions	There is a *sustained focus* on **knowledge questions** connected to the prescribed title and are well chosen – **developed** with *investigation* of **different perspectives** and **linked** *effectively* to **areas of knowledge** and/or **ways of knowing**.	There is a *focus* on **knowledge questions** *connected* to the prescribed title – **developed** with *acknowledgement* of **different perspectives** and **linked** to **areas of knowledge** and/or **ways of knowing**.
Quality of analysis of knowledge questions	**Arguments** are *clear*, supported by **real-life examples** and are *effectively evaluated*; **counterclaims** are extensively *explored*; implications are *drawn*.	Arguments are *clear*, supported by **real-life examples** and are *evaluated*; some **counterclaims** are identified and *explored*.

The essay assesses your understanding and analysis of knowledge questions.

Analysing claims and counter-claims

Your essay is an analysis of knowledge questions. You can approach a knowledge question by looking at all sides of the argument and assessing the foundations and basis of each of those claims and arguments. Counter-claims need to be extensively explored.

If claims and counter-claims are used improperly in an essay, it could result in nothing more than a mixture of different views. There are a number of ways you can use claims and counter-claims to develop good analysis:

- Consider the *strengths and weaknesses* of claims.
- Identify hidden *assumptions* behind the claims.

Keep notes on claims and counter-claims made in your TOK lessons. TOK is not separate from your learning in other lessons, and subject-specific debates can be a great potential source of TOK examples. In art, a debate could be over whether classical art is less or more meaningful than modern art, or in science over what are the most important unanswered questions or 'known unknowns' are. In biology it could be to explain why we have so few genes. Or in physics it could be our limited understanding of dark matter and dark energy. You can use your experience of these subject-specific debates as a resource to draw on: weigh up the knowledge claims and counter-claims, and consider the basis and grounds for them.

Task: think about

How do we know if it is justified to classify something as 'a great work of art'?
Knowledge claim: 'Great art' may give us insights that have been accepted as true across a number of cultures, and the arts can 'tell us a shared truth' that transcends time and culture.
Counter-claim: Art is produced at a particular time and in a particular culture and great art is culturally relative.

Weigh up the claims:
- Think of examples of artworks that could be used to support either the knowledge claim or counter-claim, for example Beethoven's symphonies, the poetry of Rabindranath Tagore, Picasso's art, or the works of Shakespeare.
- Which, if either, of the claims above are you most persuaded by and why?
- Is a great work of art similar to or different from a great work of science, literature, spirituality or mathematics?
- If you accept one of the claims, what impact might that argument have in other areas of knowledge?
- Consider a third possibility, a synthesis between the claim and the counter-claim.

Using examples to sharpen the analysis

Your essay needs to focus on analysis rather than description. Examples can be used to support your analysis. One approach is to use an example to illustrate a claim, argument or a counter-claim, as in the following:

There are some things that are beautiful that are not art, for example a sunset or a horse in full gallop, and there are some things that could be classified as art which people do not consider beautiful. One criterion for a masterpiece is that it has an enduring value, for example the Statue of Liberty, or Michelangelo's David. If it is claimed that a masterpiece has to have stood the test of time, it follows that it is too early to know if Kapoor and Balmond's Arcelor Mittal Orbit sculpture at the Olympic Park, London, will be added to this category of masterpieces. In the meantime, however, there are criteria we can use to judge the competence, skill and value of a work of art.

One criterion for judging art is that it has an enduring value. Support the analytical points you make using real-life examples.

There are some pitfalls to watch out for. Never use pointless examples that display information and description rather than analysis. Also avoid making claims which are broad generalisations, such as 'There's no agreement about what truth means and, because there's no one definition, it's impossible for anyone to claim that they know what the truth is.' Instead make comparative points that make TOK connections: 'Ethics may help us know more about values than mathematics does: "knowing how" to treat others with respect is different from "knowing how" to solve a quadratic equation, but both areas of knowledge make claims about truth.'

Giving your own opinion

Knower's perspective refers to your own view and opinion, and this is an important part of TOK. As we have seen so far, this will involve weighing up claims, arguments, counter-claims and evidence. In the process of weighing up and evaluating you can give *your own opinion* and say what you think about the relative merits of different claims and arguments. Make sure that you support your ideas with reasons.

There are different ways that you can include your own knower's perspective in your essay:

- Use your own view to weigh up a knowledge claim or counter-claim.
- Use your own personal experience or personal example to make an analytical point.

Identifying assumptions

One way that you can show your analytical skills is to identify assumptions. However, assumptions can be so well hidden that they can be difficult to spot. Your essay needs to show that you can identify hidden assumptions behind knowledge claims. For example, here are two common assumptions:

1 There is a deep conflict between science and religion.
2 The arts are relevant only on a personal level and contain no knowledge at all.

Looking 'behind' these claims reveals that neither of them stand up to much scrutiny. The first one might be based on an assumption about the scope of religion. If we see the scope of religion in terms of ethics, religion offers guidance on how to live rather than a concrete set of beliefs and does not necessarily conflict directly with science. Alvin Plantinga, in *Where the Conflict Really Lies: Science, Religion, and Naturalism* (2011), puts the case for there being only a superficial conflict between religion and science, but a deep conflict between religion and naturalism.

For the second statement, in many cultures art is very public and relevant on a shared level, as shown by art galleries, theatres and music concerts. The insights communicated by the arts might count as a type of shared knowledge.

Considering implications

Implications are more than consequences. By implications we mean thinking through the line of reasoning to what comes next or what follows. You might consider the implications of claims by looking beyond them and thinking what follows from them. This requires you to evaluate the degree of consistency in your thinking; if we turn one cog it might affect other cogs or other areas of knowledge. Our conclusion in one subject area may have an impact in other areas.

---

knower's perspective: your own personal viewpoint

You can show your knower's perspective by using examples from that reflect your own experience and learning from your IB subjects or from CAS.

Try and avoid using examples from this or other TOK books; your own examples will reflect your own voice.

Assumptions can be implicit and well hidden or explicit and more obvious.

Avoid making common assumptions such as 'we don't know much in the human sciences because people are unpredictable'. Consider the counter argument here; experiments in the human sciences can establish patterns of behaviour.

Another common assumption is that 'moral judgements are relative'. The implication is that 'anything goes'. Consider the counter argument that there are some things that are absolutely wrong; such as the use of torture.

Think along these lines:

If it is the case that x, it follows that y ...

If it is the case that the theories of general relativity and quantum mechanics compete with each other, it follows that our shared knowledge in science cannot claim to be complete or entirely coherent.

You could develop this by considering how this argument applies to other areas of knowledge. If our shared scientific knowledge is incomplete, how far is this also the case in other areas of knowledge?

If it is the case that x, it does not follow that y ...

If it is the case that the arts are open to interpretation, it doesn't follow that any interpretation of art is acceptable.

You could develop this by considering if it is the case that there are limits to what is an acceptable interpretation in other areas of knowledge.

> Identifying the assumptions and considering the implications of claims and arguments will demonstrate your skills of analysis.

Task: activity

Identify the assumptions behind and implications beyond these personal knowledge claims.

1 I think that indigenous communities know how to live in harmony with the environment.
2 There should be no limit to our imagination in the arts, history and science.
3 I believe that students should not have to pay fees for their university education.
4 While flipping a coin I intuitively feel that it has a bias towards landing on heads rather than tails.
5 I know what my first memory was.
6 I know that religious knowledge systems can offer individuals knowledge of what is holy and sacred.
7 My faith in God inspires me to behave in a way that is kind and honest.
8 I hope to achieve more than 30 points in my IB Diploma.
9 I have heard that the fate of every species including our own is to one day become extinct.
10 I have an intuitive feeling that my freedom is an illusion.

> Think about the implications beyond knowledge claims and arguments. If it is the case that *x*, what follows? If we turn one cog how might it affect other areas? How might our conclusion in one area have an impact in other areas?

Task: think about

Consider the implications of the following. For each statement discuss your response.

- If we accept the argument that mathematics and science are the most certain areas of knowledge, does it follow that knowledge in the arts has less value?
- If knowledge of right and wrong varies from person to person, does it follow that any behaviour is acceptable?
- If we have a tendency to accept only evidence that conforms to our existing view of the world (confirmation bias) does it follow that someone can never really appreciate views that differ from their own?
- If our notion of beauty is determined by our particular culture and historical context, does it follow that no-one will agree about what is beautiful?
- If art teaches us something about ourselves, human nature or the human condition, does it follow that the arts are more useful in this respect than other areas of knowledge?
- If I am internationally minded, does it follow that I should be committed to a particular set of ethical values? If so, what are they?

> In your own essay, consider the assumptions behind and implications beyond your own argument.

Widening your analysis

Practical tips for sharpening the analysis using the knowledge framework

The knowledge framework is outlined in Unit 2, Chapter 4. You can make use of it to sharpen your analysis in essays. As we have seen, there are five parts to the knowledge framework:

1 Scope and applications
2 Specific terminology and concepts
3 Methods used to produce knowledge
4 Key historical developments
5 Links with personal knowledge

For example, you might compare the *scope and applications* of religious knowledge systems with those of science or you might compare the *concept* of truth in mathematics with that in ethics. Make use of the framework so that you can make connections and comparisons between areas of knowledge.

Here is an example of how you might compare the methods used to gain knowledge in science and history:

> Scientific knowledge can be tested experimentally, whereas historical knowledge is 'tested' against an interpretation of the evidence. Both methods make use of a hypothesis to make observations about the past or present, but it doesn't follow that the methods in history and science are equally useful or lead to equally certain knowledge. Knowledge claims that are falsified in science can lead to new knowledge, and new schools of thought in history can make us think in new ways about the past.

Using links and connections

Use the knowledge framework to think about the *similarities, differences, connections* and *links* between different areas of knowledge.

One technique to develop your analysis in an essay is to take the *key concept* in the title (in this case, truth, but it could be 'explanation' or 'evidence') and to consider its different meanings. 'To what extent is the truth different in mathematics, the arts and ethics?' was one of the prescribed titles set in November 2009 and May 2010. Consider different definitions of the key concept, truth, and use the different interpretations as a way of introducing analysis into your essay.

- If by truth we mean **shared knowledge** that most people believe, it follows that …
- If by truth we mean **personal knowledge** that is true for me, it follows that …
- If by truth we mean knowledge claims that have been scientifically tested and have *not been falsified* it follows that …
- If by truth we mean what matches the world, it follows that …
- If by truth we mean what fits in with what I already know, it follows that …

> ℹ The distinction between shared and personal knowledge is explored in Unit 1, Chapter 3.

> ★ You can develop your analysis further by using examples that would and examples that would not support that definition of the concept (truth).

In an essay you might make the following points:

1 I would classify some things as art which I do not consider to be beautiful.
2 In order to know something I need evidence.
3 I am the master of my memory and I select memories that fit in with the story that I want to tell about myself.
4 Models and maps have important applications but cannot represent our knowledge with much accuracy.
5 There is a difference between my 'faith that' something is the case and my 'faith in' something.
6 Paradigm shifts change our preconceptions and bring about new knowledge.
7 Different societies share some moral principles, despite their cultural differences.
8 Our beliefs are not always based on a good understanding of probability.
    a Think of several examples that could be used to support each of these points.
    b Think of several examples that would not support each of these points.
    c Rewrite, modify or change the wording of each point so that it reflects your own thinking.

Using evidence

Weighing up documentary evidence in history or evaluating evidence for an economic theory are subject-specific skills. In the context of your TOK essay, you might also weigh up and evaluate evidence relating to a knowledge claim. Consider the essay title 'To what extent does our language determine what we know?'

There might be a number of positions you could adopt and a variety of evidence to support each of them. Your essay might explore these different branches, weigh up the evidence and assess the relative merits of each:

1 Is there strong evidence to support the view that our language shapes how we think, based on the idea of linguistic determinism and the Sapir–Whorf hypothesis?
2 Is there is weak or limited evidence to support this view?
3 Is there evidence to suggest that language only communicates our knowledge; it does not determine what we can know?

You could examine the evidence for each position and reach a judgement about which evidence is most convincing.

> Recognising the alternative viewpoints will help your essay and show that you have considered different perspectives on the same knowledge question.

How might your response to an essay title be affected by your upbringing, age, social status, profession, gender, culture, historical era or intellectual background?

The IB Mission Statement includes aiming to 'encourage students across the world to become active, compassionate and lifelong learners who understand that other people, with their differences, can also be right'. (IB Mission Statement). By exploring different cultural perspectives in your essay you can consider the relative merits of a range of different viewpoints. This doesn't mean you take an uncritical approach and have to agree with everyone. Arrive at your own conclusion, having thought for yourself and considered different positions on the question and the different cultural perspectives.

Bringing in different perspectives and finding a coherent position

Depending on the essay title, you may be able to investigate an event with global significance from different perspectives. For example, if you were writing about a prescribed title to do with our knowledge in history, you might consider what we know about recent conflicts in the Middle East, taking into account the different perspectives. In Syria the uprising against President Bashar al-Assad's government began in March 2011. You could investigate the perspectives held by supporters of the President and his opponents such as the Free Syrian Army, along with the views and response of the international community and the United Nations Security Council. You might also consider the role of social media in the course of events and how perspectives are shaped by global communications and the internet.

When you write, think about how else you might look at the essay title. Show that you can investigate different perspectives, and communicate your insight that your knowledge is dependent on many variables. Show an awareness of the social, cultural and intellectual factors that shape what we know. Self-awareness includes the idea that your own perspective is one of many.

It is important to develop your own coherent position from the array of possible answers. You need to have a sound justification for your view and support your position with good reasons. Bring in your own *knower's perspective*. Here is an example of how you might express your own coherent view in an essay. 'To what extent do we need evidence to support our beliefs in different areas of knowledge?' (November 2010 and May 2011).

> <u>Knowledge claim:</u> Some people might claim that evidence is not needed in the arts, since any interpretation of the visual and literary arts is acceptable.
>
> <u>Counter-claim:</u> However, this claim doesn't stand up to scrutiny. The fact that there are prizes awarded for literary fiction and art suggest that there are standards that can be used to judge the arts. Judgements could be made on the basis of evidence in a text.
>
> <u>My own position:</u> It follows that there might be some interpretations of art that are plainly wrong; if someone thought the 'Mona Lisa' depicted a zebra they would be wrong as there is no evidence on which to base their judgement. I believe that art and literary critics are worth listening to since their opinions are based on expertise and they have a good knowledge of the context of a painting or a work of literary fiction. I think that there are some standards of judgement, but it would be acceptable if a person disagreed with what these standards were and had their own opinion and evidence to support their own beliefs.

In your essay consider different positions you can take on the question. Weigh up the merits of these positions, make a sound judgement and arrive at your own conclusion. In TOK judgement is key.

The attributes listed in the IB learner profile have connections with TOK. Which attributes of the learner profile do you think are most relevant in TOK?

As a 'risk-taker', in what ways might you take an intellectual risk? In what ways do the attributes such as 'principled' and 'caring' have an ethical dimension? To what extent does open-mindedness imply tolerance?

Summary

Analysis, links and comparisons

The following checklist sets out some of the ingredients that make up a good TOK essay. Aim to include these features in your essays.

Analysis, links and comparisons
• Understand command words and key concepts in the title.
• Make analytical rather than descriptive points.
• Use examples and counter-examples to make analytical points.
Analyse:
• Weigh up knowledge claims and counter-claims.
• Weigh up and evaluate evidence.
• Identify the similarities and differences between areas of knowledge.
• Make connections using the knowledge framework.
• Identify assumptions.
• Consider implications.

Further reading and sources

Deutscher, Guy. *'Does your language shape how you think?'* New York Times, 26 August 2010.
Available at: www.nytimes.com/2010/08/29/magazine/29language-t.html
Plantinga, Alvin. 2011. *'Where the Conflict Really Lies: Science, Religion, and Naturalism.'* Oxford University Press.

15 Developing a thesis and constructing an argument

Introduction

This chapter sets out to get you started on planning and writing your essay. We will look at developing a thesis and a strong line of argument.

The following examples are possible templates that could be adapted to construct your own argument. There are many possible structures including organisation of your ideas by area of knowledge, by theme, by perspective, or by interpretation of key concept. We will explore this further using the following prescribed title:

- To what extent is the truth different in mathematics, the arts and ethics? (May 2010)

The title invites you to explore the ways in which truth is different in three areas of knowledge. Truth might be interpreted in terms of 'tests for truth', personal truth, shared truth, abstract truth, invented truth or discovered truth. You could play around with the following structures and combine them in your own way.

1 *By area of knowledge*: mathematics, ethics, the arts. This structure can produce an excellent essay if it includes a good level of analysis.
2 *By concepts and theme*: scope and applications, theory and methodology. This structure takes concepts and examines each in relation to the knowledge question.
3 *By knowledge question*: this structure addresses the title by looking at the first connected knowledge question and its analysis, and then the second relevant knowledge question and its analysis.
4 *By thesis, antithesis and synthesis*: this structure looks at the first possibility (the case for), the second possibility or antithesis (the case against), and a third possibility (a synthesis which establishes your own new idea).

> - Your essay should avoid the extremes of blind scepticism and blind acceptance of knowledge claims, both of which can lead to naïve and unthinking essays. Ideally your essay needs to tackle the complex and challenging grey areas in between.
> - Write at least one practice essay first.

Thesis

Your thesis statement is your answer to the knowledge question. It is possible to include your thesis either in your introduction or in your conclusion. It's important that your essay says something and your thesis statement should sum up your answer with clarity and precision.

Consider this knowledge question:

> To what extent do we need evidence to support our beliefs in different areas of knowledge?' (November 2010 and May 2011)

You could phrase your thesis in the first person:

I agree with the claim that we need evidence to support our beliefs to a significant extent. Although the concept of evidence varies in both history and science, it is a concept that underpins both areas of knowledge.

or you could phrase the same thesis in a different way:

There is stronger justification for the argument for than the argument against, since without evidence, there is very little that we can claim to know in science and history.

Either approach is acceptable.

Returning to the original prescribed title, 'To what extent is the truth different in mathematics, the arts and ethics?', a draft thesis statement might be:

I agree to a large extent, given that the word 'truth' has very different meanings in different areas of knowledge and in different contexts and real-life situations.

or a longer version might be:

I will argue that there are different types of truth in each area of knowledge: there are clear differences between the truth of a solution to a quadratic equation, the truth of Tolstoy's novel 'War and Peace' and the truth value of our shared human rights.

If your title invites you to agree or disagree with a knowledge claim you might not want to agree or disagree entirely. You could agree but with conditions or reservations. For example, your thesis could be, 'although x is more logical, it is based on claims that have weak justification', or 'although x is more convincing on the surface, there is better justification for y'. You might argue that the scientific method has obvious strengths compared with methods in other areas of knowledge because any claims that are found to be false are discarded. However, you might also want to qualify your argument by claiming that 'it is a strong method based on the limited evidence available to us'.

★ Focus your time and attention on developing the quality of your argument and your thesis will follow naturally from your thought process. The thesis itself (for example, whether you agree or disagree) and its precise length are less important.

★ Your thesis may change over time as a result of thinking the knowledge question through and discussing it with your teacher and peers.

Task: activity

Choose a prescribed essay title, either from this book or from the list of six titles prescribed for your own examination session. Examples of prescribed essay titles can be found at the end of Chapters in Units 1 and 2. Write your own draft thesis statement. Sum up your answer to the title in two or three sentences.

Arguments

Essays have an **argument**, and your TOK essay can be thought of as an extended argument. That means the essay addresses the prescribed title in a way that leads to a clear conclusion. In order to get from the title to the conclusion, your essay needs to show a clear line of argument sustained throughout your essay.

When you come up with your own argument you are showing that you have understood the central concepts in the TOK course and can organise them in an original and creative way. We have already considered arguments, logic and reasoning in earlier chapters. For the conclusion to be convincing it needs to have both a true and reasonable set of *premises* and your argument needs to be *valid*. That means the logic of the statements needs to flow so that it makes sense and is coherent.

argument: a logical, coherent, compelling, precise discussion based on evidence and open to alternative perspectives

Have you evaluated your own argument? It helps to distance yourself from your own argument and weigh up its strengths and weaknesses.

Task: activity

1 Look back at the examples of prescribed essay titles at the end of Chapters in Units 1 and 2 and practise constructing an argument for one of them. Write out the stages of your argument, showing your main points and a conclusion. Take time with this and begin with a draft.

2 Write each stage of your argument on a different card and experiment with changing the order so that the argument flows coherently. You may want to take some cards out and add some new cards so that each stage of your argument follows logically.

Planning and drafting

When you are ready, begin to plan your draft essay. The point of planning is to have a clear idea of what you are going to write before you actually start writing the essay. A plan is a series of rough ideas that will form the shape of your essay. It's a good idea to focus your plan on the structure of your argument, the supporting evidence and the different perspectives you will consider. Begin with a draft argument, your sequence of ideas and develop a paragraph plan. If you aim to write around 12 paragraphs that should be about right. This is a rough guide and a few either side is fine. When you are confident that you have planned a coherent argument, begin structuring the paragraph plan for your first draft. We'll look more at the development of paragraphs in Chapter 16.

A plan should help you organise your ideas. The point of a plan is to get your ideas down on paper and then you can work on refining them.

In terms of supporting your essay writing, your teacher's role is to encourage and guide you and to ensure that the essay is your own independent work. You are allowed to discuss the essay title with your teacher and you can show them a written essay plan. You are also allowed to submit one draft essay to your teacher. They are not permitted to mark the draft but they are allowed to write one set of comments offering general feedback.

Task: activity

1 Write a first draft of your essay. As you write this first draft, focus on developing the specific features mentioned in the summary on the next page.

2 Leave the essay for a week to give you some distance from your ideas. Mark the essay yourself against the holistic criteria. Think about the quality of your argument, the sequence and structure of your ideas, links and comparisons, depth and breadth, treatment of claims and counter-claims, and your overall quality of analysis.

Summary

Analysis, links and comparisons

The following checklist sets out some of the ingredients that make up a good TOK essay. Aim to include these features in your essays.

Developing a thesis and constructing an argument

- Plan a coherent argument.
- Construct a clear thesis.
- Identify key terms.
- Use a clear sequence of ideas.
- Use evidence and key examples.
- Make a paragraph plan, approximately 12 paragraphs.
- Make a first draft, edit it and write a second draft.

16 Structure, introduction, examples and conclusion

Introduction

In this chapter we will focus on how you can structure your ideas. We outline what makes a good introduction, conclusion and an effective use of examples.

Structuring your ideas

Before you write your introduction or conclusion, check that you have a progressive argument. Your argument is a sequence of ideas that follow logically from each other. There is not one formula or framework for achieving this, and the whole point of the essay is that it is meant to demonstrate your own independent thinking. There is no 'one size fits all' structure so choose your own structure: one that fits the essay title and reflects your own critical thought.

The introduction

Don't use your opening paragraph as a 'warm-up' before you really get going. Include your own interpretation of the question and outline how you intend to approach the question. Indicate the scope of your essay and which areas of knowledge or ways of knowing you will consider. You can include your thesis statement in your introduction or conclusion. Make sure you don't interpret the question in such a way that it is so unusual it bears little relation to the set title.

Your first sentence needs to catch the reader's attention. It needs to reflect the fact that you have already thought long and hard about this question for yourself and you want to begin with something that reflects *your* thinking. Avoid beginning with dictionary definitions, which make for boring openings. A dictionary cannot get close to communicating the richness of the concepts that you will have developed over the course. Dictionary definitions are not appropriate in TOK essays because a single bland definition is unlikely to shed any light on what the concept means for your reader. You can begin with a clearly worded statement that forms the first of your original thoughts.

Avoid starting like this: 'Because this title raises such complex issues, we can only answer this question after careful consideration of the alternative perspectives.' The examiner knows this already and your task is to shed light on

> ⭐ Instead of using a dictionary definition, consider explaining what you mean by the key term and use examples to illustrate what you mean. This is often more appropriate than offering a closed dictionary definition.
>
> In the introduction you can set out the scope of your essay and offer your own position.

what the complex issues are and say something about what the perspectives might reveal. Instead, consider saying something interesting about the issues or the perspectives you will be considering.

Paragraphs

Your paragraphs need to flow so that each of them develops and illuminates your ideas further as the essay progresses. Your paragraphs need to mirror your argument, so that each one follows logically on to the next.

Don't include too many ideas in a single paragraph and change paragraph when moving on to a new, important point. It's a useful technique to begin each paragraph with a topic sentence that indicates the theme of your paragraph. For example, 'Varying degrees of truth are given by an academic study of a historical event and a novel based around a historical theme.'

You can show that you are taking a new direction in your argument by using phrases that make the transitions clear to your reader: 'While this may apply to ethical theories, we also need to consider scientific theories …' or 'On the other hand, methods used to gain knowledge in the human sciences …' or 'Having considered the strengths of the arguments for …'

Task: activity

1 Choose one of the essay titles below.
  a Discuss the roles of language and reason in history. (May 2011)
  b 'There are no absolute distinctions between what is true and what is false.' Discuss this claim. (May 2011)
  c Examine the ways empirical evidence should be used to make progress in different areas of knowledge. (May 2010)
2 Using your chosen essay title, experiment with different structures. Make a draft plan that structures your ideas by area of knowledge, theme or perspective.
3 Write two possible introductions, one that you think will achieve high marks and one that you think would obtain low marks. Show them to your teacher, discuss them and think about the ingredients that you need to include in an effective introduction.
4 Look at the introductions to some exemplar essays and compare the different approaches.
5 Using an exemplar essay, identify the topic/theme of each paragraph. Use this to look at the flow of the paragraphs. How do the paragraphs effectively move the argument on? Look at the use of topic sentences and transitions.

Style

A suitable style for writing your essay is neither too personal and casual nor too dry and formal. The chatty tone of someone's diary is not appropriate for a TOK essay. An inappropriate style would be: 'To coin a phrase used by my Aunty Jennifer, "life's what you make it"; we talk about all sorts of interesting things like the meaning of life.' Avoid this kind of irrelevant waffling.

Also avoid a writing style that attempts to copy an academic style but which has no substance and confuses the reader. This verbose style is inappropriate: 'In his book *X*, the writer *Y* expatiates on a controversial, infamous and improbable thesis which I doubt would stand up to any significant scrutiny …'

The final essay needs to be submitted double-spaced in 12 point font. The spaces between your lines enable the examiner to make comments and annotations. Use Times New Roman, Arial or another standard font.

If you adopt an analytical style somewhere between extremes, which feels comfortable and natural, this should be about right. The other examples used in this chapter reflect a more appropriate style. At all costs make sure that you use clear language that communicates your meaning precisely.

Think carefully about your use of 'I' and 'we'. In TOK it can be appropriate to make use of the first person and mention 'I' and 'we' to distinguish between personal and shared knowledge. However, an alternative approach is to mention 'I' only in the conclusion when you are drawing the strands of your argument together. Your essay can take either approach but be sure to use *precise language*. You want your voice to be authentically yours but also clear.

Examples

Examples based on real-life situations serve to illustrate the points you want to make in your essay. Choose authentic examples that are fresh and make your own voice clear. The source of your examples might be class notes, books, TV documentaries, radio programmes or internet sources. Examples can function in a number of ways.

They can be used to illustrate an argument or counter-argument, or to illustrate personal knowledge and shared knowledge. Remember that the examiner reading your essay might live anywhere in the world. If you use an example that might only make sense to people with a similar cultural perspective, make sure that you explain it clearly.

Avoid using examples that are caricatures or stereotypes, such as: 'There is a truth behind the claim that it is wrong to kill, for example all religions agree that it is wrong.' This is a descriptive example which does not support analysis. Examples need to be real, concrete, specific and used to support some analysis of knowledge claims:

> The principle that all life is sacred might be shared by some religions, but how that principle applies in real-life situations might differ even between people belonging to the same faith. Abortion and euthanasia, for example, might divide opinion between Christians, but an individual Christian might come to their own conclusion about moral issues by combining their faith and reason together. Looking behind the claim that 'it is wrong to kill' is the assumption that all life should be preserved . . .

⭐ Use examples to illustrate a range of things from analytical points, knowledge claims, counter-claims, arguments, counter-arguments, shared or personal knowledge.

In 2010, The Clay Mathematics Institute in the US awarded a Millennium Prize to the Russian mathematician, Dr Grigori Perelman, for solving the Poincaré conjecture. What analytical points might this example illustrate?

Task: think about

Consider this list of real-life examples. What analytical point could each example be used to illustrate?

- A cleaner's mop and bucket is left in an art gallery by accident and the next day people think that it is art.
- A Clay Millennium Mathematics Prize is won by a mathematician who has found a solution to a long-standing mathematics problem.
- The Dalai Lama is described as a spiritual genius.
- A man is busking on a street and no-one recognises that he is actually one of the world's best violinists.
- The Higgs boson particle (the most elementary particle believed to exist) is discovered.

The conclusion

Your conclusion needs to do two things: give both a summary and an evaluation. Make sure that you have answered the question directly. Check that your conclusion is consistent with what you have argued in the essay.

Avoid weak endings that sum up with something like: 'Having looked at all the difficulties with answering the question we have to accept that scientists and historians need to agree to disagree.' That type of ending tells the examiner nothing, and such a conclusion suggests that more time and effort is needed to go into constructing a good argument. End with a view that points forwards to an evaluation of your own argument and any further knowledge questions that lie outside the scope of your essay.

Avoiding plagiarism

It's absolutely necessary that this essay is your own work. It needs to show your ideas, your skills and your understanding. It's the one essay you will write where your judgement really counts. Make a clear distinction between your own ideas and those of other people. There are a number of ways you can do this.

Paraphrase: acknowledge the author and express the gist of their claims in your own words. 'In his book *The Origin and Goal of History*, Karl Jaspers puts forward the concept of an Axial Period, the idea of an axis or dividing line in world history, around 500 BCE.'

Use quotations: you can quote other people's ideas by putting text in single or double quotation marks. The reference in brackets is a way of indicating a book mentioned in the bibliography: 'Karl Jaspers claims that the purpose of his book is "to assist in heightening our awareness of the present". (Jaspers, 1953).'

'I have gathered a garland of other men's flowers, and nothing is mine but the cord that binds them.'
Michel de Montaigne (1533–92)

Check that every sentence you use counts. Avoid any statements of the obvious as they have no function. Avoid truisms as they are likely to contribute nothing valuable to your essay (unless you are using them to make a critical point).

Referencing: You need to cite any written or visual sources that you use. The IB does not specify one way of doing this. A standard way is to add footnotes/endnotes or a list of references that are cited in the text.
In your bibliography set out any books or articles you have used following a consistent and conventional method, for example, author, title of source, publisher, date, with relevant page numbers if appropriate: S. Law, *The Philosophy Gym: 25 Short Adventures in Thinking* (Headline Book Publishing, 2004) For web-based sources you should include the URL address and the date of access.

The IB publishes 50 excellent essays which can be purchased online at the IB store. It's worth spending time reading some of these to get an idea of what makes an excellent essay. The titles will not be the same as those on your list of prescribed titles but the essays will fulfil similar tasks within a similar word limit. The aim is never to copy what other students have done, but instead to get an idea of what it is possible to achieve.

Task: activity

1 Read an exemplar essay that your teacher can access from the IB Online Curriculum Centre (OCC) and award it marks against the holistic criteria.
2 Compare your comments with those made by examiners.

Summary

Analysis, links and comparisons

The following checklist sets out some of the ingredients that make up a good TOK essay. Aim to include these features in your essays.

Structure, introduction, examples and conclusion

- Structure your ideas.
- Use paragraphs to take your argument forward.
- Use an appropriate writing style.
- Make precise use of 'I' and 'we'.
- Use clear language.
- Define your terms but avoid dictionary definitions.
- Use specific concrete examples based on real-life situations.
- Avoid examples that caricature or stereotype.
- Use examples to make analytical points and to illustrate knowledge claims, arguments, shared and personal knowledge.
- Write a suitable introduction.
- Include a summary and evaluation in your conclusion.
- Never plagiarise.
- Make a clear distinction between your own ideas and other people's ideas.

Final checklist

Use these questions as a final checklist. This is a rough guide. Every essay title is unique and there are many ways of answering a question. When planning your response to an essay title you will be on the right track if you have considered some of these questions.

1 What are the connected knowledge questions?

2 What are the different ways of answering the question that are relevant to TOK?

3 How is the knowledge question related to ways of knowing, and areas of knowledge?

4 What is my thesis statement?

5 How does my argument develop?

6 Have I weighed up knowledge claims and evidence?

7 Have I extensively explored counter-claims?

8 Have I used suitable real-life examples?

9 What impact might my conclusion have in related areas of the TOK diagram?

10 In what ways might I use the knowledge framework to support my analysis of the question?

11 Have I identified assumptions and considered implications?

12 Have I explored other perspectives and different ways of looking at the question?

17 Understanding the assessment requirements

Introduction

Towards the end of your TOK course you will give a presentation that will be formally assessed. It is likely to take place in the familiar context of your TOK class and you will be assessed by your teacher. You will be assessed on how well you can apply TOK thinking to real life. The point of a TOK presentation is to make links between the abstract world of critical thinking and ordinary everyday situations. This chapter sets out to explain the holistic marking criteria that will be used to judge the quality of your presentation and offer some practical tips for choosing a topic.

The purpose of the presentation

The final assessed presentation that you give is **summative**. This means that it assesses what you have learnt during the course. However, it helps to have plenty of practice along the way. A formal practice presentation at some point in the course is very helpful. So too are mini, informal presentations that will form part of regular classwork. There are suggested presentation tasks at the end of chapters in Units 1 and 2. However, the IB specifies that the same material, whether it is the same real-life situation or knowledge question, can be assessed only once.

The presentation is also intended to be part of your intellectual journey. It offers you a chance to relate TOK to the real world and to demonstrate your critical thinking skills. It is the result of your own independent thoughts, TOK insights and conclusions. It is about your own **knower's perspective**. In this way it will benefit the rest of the class, who will learn more about TOK as a result of seeing your presentation. In this way it is also a **formative** learning experience for your class.

IB assessment

Your presentation score makes up one-third of your total marks for TOK. Like the essay, the presentation does not assess your research skills. It assesses your analysis of a knowledge question that arises from a single real life situation. However, unlike the essay, you formulate your own knowledge question.

summative: summative assessment *of learning* measures learning outcomes, and your performance at the end of a topic or course of study; an example is your final IB exams in November or May

knower's perspective: your own viewpoint

formative: formative assessment *for learning* informs and shapes your learning during a topic or course of study; an example is your teacher's feedback on a practice essay and suggestions for how you can further improve your writing skills

> ## Do(es) the presenter(s) succeed in showing how TOK concepts can have practical application?

> ### Has the student:

- described clearly the real-life situation that forms the launching point for the presentation?
- extracted and clearly formulated a single knowledge question from the real-life situation?
- identified and explored various perspectives in relation to the knowledge question, and deployed examples and arguments in the service of this exploration?
- related the findings of and insights from the analysis back to the chosen real-life situation and showed how they might be relevant to other real-life situations?

The presentation assesses how well you can apply TOK thinking, concepts and ideas.

Your presentation is marked using a holistic approach. The level you are awarded will be based on the overall global impression of your presentation. Your presentation will be awarded one of five levels depending on its quality, with 5 being the highest level and 1 the lowest. There are descriptions for each level published by the IB and you will need to keep a copy of these. There are 10 marks in total for your presentation, and your mark will depend upon the level you achieve. The level descriptors suggest features that are typical of a presentation at that level and should not be misunderstood as a shopping list of essential features.

The following table is based on information given in the IB subject guide.

Level 5 (top level)	9–10 marks (maximum marks)
Level 4	7–8 marks
Level 3	5–6 marks
Level 2	3–4 marks
Level 1	1–2 marks
	0 marks

You can choose whether you give your presentation individually or in a group of two or a maximum of three people. As a rule of thumb, individuals have 10 minutes each so if you are presenting on your own aim to give a 10-minute presentation, for pairs it's 20 minutes and for groups of three it's 30 minutes. It is expected that everyone in a group is awarded the same mark so it's important that everyone does their fair share of the preparation and delivery.

Your presentation can take a number of forms. Use your imagination and think about how you can get your points across using a variety of techniques. It could take the form of a talk, a dialogue, a sketch, an interview or a debate. It doesn't

The IB TOK subject guide sets out what is required in a presentation and essay. Keep your own copy of the subject guide. It is available for your teacher on the Online Curriculum Centre.

have to take the form of a PowerPoint presentation. The IB specifies that you are not allowed to read from a script or an essay. Your presentation must be delivered 'live' to the class and cannot be pre-recorded.

It is a requirement that before your presentation you fill in a form, the IB 'presentation planning document' TK/PPD Form (presentation and marking form). This is a two-sided form with questions and you complete your response to the questions using no more than 500 words in 12 point font. Submit this document to your teacher before the presentation. Your teacher will add comments. The presentation and the TK/PPD Form are both internally assessed. Schools will standardise their own internal marking, and your form might be externally moderated. Your teacher will watch your presentation and award you a mark against the holistic criteria. Afterwards you are required to mark your own work too. Your mark does not affect the teacher's mark.

Level 5 Excellent 9–10	Level 4 Very good 7–8
The presentation is focused on a *well-formulated* **knowledge question** that is *clearly connected* to a *specified* **real-life situation**. The knowledge question is *effectively explored* in the context of the real-life situation, using *convincing* **arguments**, with *investigation* of *different* **perspectives**. The **outcomes of the analysis** are shown to be *significant to the chosen real-life situation and to others*.	The presentation is focused on a **knowledge question** that is *connected* to a *specified* **real-life situation**. The knowledge question is *explored* in the context of the real-life situation, using *clear* **arguments**, with *acknowledgement* of *different* **perspectives**. The **outcomes of the analysis** are shown to be *significant to the real-life situation*.

The presentation assesses how well you can apply TOK thinking.

TOK concepts and real-life situations

In the presentation you are expected to apply TOK to a real-life situation. One way of doing this is to look for TOK in everyday life. Here are some examples of suitable real-life situations.

1   The first example is an idea that arose from a student's personal experience while reading an article about Aung San Suu Kyi, the Burmese pro-democracy leader. She was released in November 2010, having spent many years as a political prisoner under house arrest in Burma, now Myanmar. The student read about how her campaign for democracy and human rights had led her to win the Nobel Peace Prize in 1991, and the student began thinking about the contribution that individuals can make to promote peace and justice, how far we act in our own self-interest and how far we have an ethical responsibility to help others.

    www.nobelprize.org/nobel_prizes/peace/laureates/1991/kyi.html

2   The second example comes from a leaflet about breast cancer that a student picked up and read at a doctors' surgery. Among women who drink at least 1 unit of alcohol every day, 12 out of 100 are likely to develop breast cancer; among women who do not drink alcohol, only 11 out of every 100 will develop breast cancer. So we know that not drinking alcohol reduces the risk of developing breast cancer by 1 in 100. But how might an understanding of probability affect the way we behave? Might women be inclined to give up alcohol to decrease the odds of getting breast cancer in their lifetime?

3   The third example is from a student who was inspired by a school assembly. The student was interested to learn more about the Arab Spring, a series of anti-government protests in the Middle East which began in December 2010 and has led to political leaders being deposed in countries such as Tunisia, Egypt, Libya and Yemen, civil unrest, and in some countries, civil war. The student was keen to discover what has caused these events, in what ways the events were connected, and how social media and the internet played a role. The student began thinking about the way that our knowledge is shaped by reports in the news and how our knowledge of historical events might be linked to emotion, memory and language.

    www.bbc.co.uk/news/world-middle-east-12813859
    www.un.org/en/sc/

With your presentation, your teacher's role is to support and guide you. You are allowed to have up to three meetings with your teacher in which you can discuss the real-life situation, the knowledge question and the structure of your presentation. However, your presentation must be your own independent work. With your teacher you need to agree a date and time to give your presentation allowing yourself sufficient time to prepare.

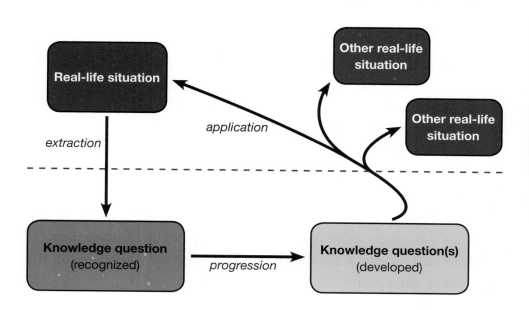

When you plan a presentation use the structure given in the diagram shown here.
    The level 'above' the line represents the ordinary 'real world' and this is where your presentation begins, with a real-life situation. The level 'below' the line represents the abstract work of TOK thinking where your knowledge question belongs.

The presentation diagram offers a useful structure for planning your presentation.

There are many sources of real-life situations. Choose one from your own experience of learning. Keep a record of real-life situations from your six IB subjects that you could use as the starting point for your TOK presentation.

Examples 1 and 2 show the types of notes you could make on potential real-life situations. You could develop these into a TOK presentation.

Task: think about

Think about some real-life situations from your own experience. A real-life situation can be any situation that has made you think. Real-life situations might arise from:

- your own thoughts and ideas
- conversations with people
- discussions or examples from your TOK class or other IB subjects or CAS activities
- books, websites, newspapers, chat rooms, magazines, journals
- lectures, films, TV programmes, DVDs.

These are examples of students' notes that have been taken about real-life situations and the general questions that arise from them. These ideas are good starting points for planning a presentation. Notice the way that they are personal and fresh. The examples reflect the students' personal experience. However, these examples show starting points; they are not intended to be fully formed TOK examples. We follow up these examples in Chapter 19 on page 156 to show how they can be developed.

Example 1

I saw a documentary about Japanese macaques (snow monkeys) who live in such cold conditions that they need to keep warm in thermal springs, the human equivalent of a hot tub. However, the male in charge only allows the 'highest-ranking' females and infants into the warm water. I started thinking about an explanation for this behaviour in terms of group memberships and identity, limited space in the pool or the idea of a 'lower-class' macaque. With more than 90% of our DNA shared with them, observing them might provoke a hard look at our own hierarchies. Why do we have 'in-groups'? Why do we have an unequal distribution of resources? I started thinking about what different subjects such as biology and psychology might tell us about the rules that animals and people live by.

Example 2

I watched a TV documentary about quantum physics. In quantum physics things occur that seem counter-intuitive. The presenters demonstrated this by showing how super-cooled liquids such as liquid helium can simply pass through a solid glass beaker. The point was to show that on a quantum level things do not behave in an obvious way. It got me thinking about how our senses may not be entirely reliable for giving us knowledge. There are limits to what we see, hear, taste, touch and smell. I also thought about how we can claim to have knowledge of things in mathematics, science and religious knowledge systems that we cannot know from our sense perception.

Summary

Key features of the presentation (see also page 167)

What the presentation is	What the presentation is not
an assessment of how well you can apply TOK concepts to ordinary real-life situations	a test of purely abstract thinking
an enquiry or investigation into a knowledge question	the delivery of information, research or a report
based on your own well-formulated knowledge question that arises naturally from a real-life situation	based only on a subject-specific question
an analysis of the knowledge question using convincing arguments and examples	a description of the knowledge question
a consideration of different perspectives on a knowledge question	just one perspective on a knowledge question
a consideration of the implications of the analysis for the real-life situation and other related situations	a conclusion with no consideration of its implications elsewhere

Assessment

Who assesses the presentation?	Internally examined by TOK teachers in school with some external moderation
How many can present?	Between 1 and 3 people
What is the time limit?	Approximately 10 minutes per individual, i.e. 30 minutes for a group of 3, 20 minutes for a pair and 10 minutes for an individual
How is the presentation marked?	Holistic / global impression marking
How much it is worth?	33% of the total marks for TOK
What is the maximum score?	10 marks in total
How is the presentation submitted?	You complete the IB 'presentation planning document' (TK/PPD Form) and submit it to your teacher. Your teacher can obtain a copy of this form from the *'Handbook of Procedures for the Diploma Programme'.* You then deliver your presentation in school. Your teacher will upload the forms after completion. Your planning form and your presentation will be internally assessed by your school and a sample of TK/PPD forms will be externally moderated by the IB.

18 Extracting a knowledge question from a real-life situation

Introduction

This chapter sets out to show you how to start planning an excellent TOK presentation. We will look in detail at formulating a knowledge question.

Real-life situations and knowledge questions

The real-life situation is the starting point for your presentation. A real-life situation can be any specific situation that has made you think about knowing or knowledge. The situation can be relevant to your local community or your school or relevant nationally or internationally. It might also be based on a subject-specific issue.

TOK provides an opportunity to reflect on knowledge questions that arise directly from your IB experience.

School issues are a suitable potential source of real-life situations. You might think about the place of knowledge in your immediate school community.

Your six IB subjects are also a source of real-life situations for presentations. Use TOK as a chance to reflect on what you know from your any of your IB courses such as your Group 1 Language, or Group 5 Mathematics and Computer Science. CAS activities can also be a source of real-life situations.

If you choose a national or international issue this is a chance to think about the role of shared knowledge in international communities. You may already have a real-life situation in mind, but if you need ideas, you might choose from one of these three areas:

1 school issues
2 national or international issues
3 subject-specific issues.

The following examples are intended to get you thinking and to show the relationship between the real-life situation and the knowledge question.

There are many possible sources of real-life situations. Consider choosing a real-life situation based on what we know in a particular academic discipline that you are studying as one of your six IB subjects. For example think about a real-life situation from your Group 4 science subject or from your study of the human sciences in Group 3.

Your teacher will mark you on the basis of your presentation planning form (TK/PPD) and the quality of your presentation. They will record their marks on the same form which will be internally moderated and a sample of these will be externally moderated by the IB.

Extracting a knowledge question from a real-life situation

1 School issues: consider issues in your school community

Real-life situation / questions	Knowledge question
Is there a school or college committee that represents your voice? What are the issues? Whose voices are heard? Are the discussions based mainly on reason or emotion? What is the basis of authority?	To what extent do 'rules' and conventions in different areas of knowledge determine what we know?
Your IB curriculum: What values does it embody? What assumptions are made? Is there flexibility? How might other educational models and different approaches compare? In what ways does the curriculum affect what you know? Are there approaches, subjects or skills that would be useful to know about?	To what extent is what we know in two areas of knowledge shaped by our culture and education?

For the TOK presentation you come up with your own knowledge question.

Notice how knowledge questions do not mention the real-life situation. When you generate your knowledge question, use TOK vocabulary and don't use the vocabulary that belongs to the real-life situation.

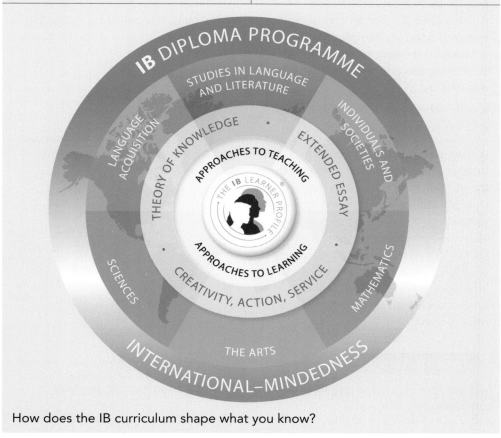

How does the IB curriculum shape what you know?

When you formulate your own knowledge question for your presentation ensure that it has these key features:

- open ended (For example , 'To what extent...?' or 'How can we know if...?' or others)
- about knowledge or knowing (explicitly mention one of these words in the question)
- expressed in TOK vocabulary (see page 154 for a list)
- comparative (explores the relationship between ways of knowing and/ or areas of knowledge)

2 National and international issues: consider issues in the national and international news

Real–life situation / questions	Knowledge question
The economies of Brazil, Russia, India and China (BRIC) are predicted to be the dominant economies of the future. Think of economic issues. Why is there a global recession? Think of explanations offered by economists. What claims are made about the problem? Does anyone have a solution?	To what extent is our knowledge in the human sciences and the natural sciences based on facts and explanations?
Xi Jinping became the leader of China's 1.3 billion people in 2013. Have there been any elections of political leaders recently or are there about to be? When people vote do they vote in their own self-interest or in the interests of others? What are the relative merits of each approach?	To what extent can we predict the outcome of an event in different subject areas?

3 Subject-specific issues: consider issues and debates in IB subjects that you study

Real–life situation / questions	Knowledge question
Think of developments in technology. Professor Kevin Warwick, an internationally renowned expert in cybernetics, became the world's first cyborg by 'enhancing' his sense perception. Is this example repellent or attractive and why? Is your response governed more by emotion, intuition, faith or reason?	To what extent is our sense perception a reliable source of knowledge in history, the arts and science?
Interdisciplinarity involves combining subjects together in new and relevant ways. Consider the approach in the UK to single-subject university degrees (say Single Honours History) alongside the liberal arts approach in the US and new interdisciplinary degrees in the UK, such as the Arts and Sciences (BASc) degree at University College, London and the BA Liberal Arts degree at King's College, London. Which subjects would you like to combine in new and relevant ways?	To what extent is it justified to claim that areas of knowledge are distinct?

Task: activity

Once you have chosen your real-life situation, write down one or two possible knowledge questions to go with it.

Formulating and developing a knowledge question

Your real-life situation could arise from reading a magazine article about the International Space Station (ISS). Your interest has been captured and now you need to think about how you can develop the real-life situation into a knowledge question. The ISS is a great example of scientific achievement, endeavour and international cooperation, but what are the knowledge questions? One approach is to think next of how it relates to ways of knowing or areas of knowledge. In this case you could apply TOK thinking in relation to the *imagination* and *reason* used by the team of international scientists to put it up in space.

You could phrase a knowledge question in the following way: 'How far is the scientific achievement of the ISS a product of international cooperation, reason and imagination?' This would make an interesting presentation, but be careful as this is still too subject-specific and not yet a well-formulated knowledge question. A knowledge question should not mention your real-life situation, and this one does mention the ISS. A well-formed knowledge question is more *general, open-ended, comparative* and explicitly about *knowing and knowledge*.

Play around with the phrasing of the question until you come up with a possible knowledge question. A better formulated knowledge question would be: 'Can we be sure that our scientific knowledge relies more on our reason than our imagination?'

It is easy to miss the point and give an engaging presentation on an interesting topic and somehow bypass the analysis of a knowledge question. If your real-life situation is about the death penalty and your knowledge question is 'How do we know if history and ethics can inform judgements about capital punishment?' it sounds like TOK because it's about knowing and two areas of knowledge. However, this is another example of a poorly formed question because it mentions the real-life situation in the knowledge question. As the question is poorly formulated, the presentation risks being on the topic of capital punishment rather than focused on knowledge. The question needs to be better formulated if it is to be a genuine analysis of a knowledge question. Always avoid using the vocabulary of your real-life situation (in this case the death penalty / capital punishment) in your knowledge question.

A clearly phrased knowledge question would be more general and would not mention the real-life situation: 'How can we know if there is certain knowledge in history and ethics?' This modified question includes the key concept 'certain knowledge'. The question is now focused on knowledge and it is still explicitly connected to the real-life situation.

> There are many examples of knowledge questions throughout this book. For assessment purposes knowledge questions need to be closely defined as suggested here.
>
> Remember that the presentation is not a report or a description; it must be focused on an analysis of a knowledge question.

TOK vocabulary

In your presentation you need to develop a knowledge question from a real-life situation. The presentation diagram (see page 147) offers a useful structure for planning and developing your ideas. Notice that there are two distinct vocabularies:

1 the vocabulary of the 'real world' and the real-life situation
2 the vocabulary of the 'TOK world' of abstract questions, concepts and critical thinking.

Your knowledge question and its analysis needs to be phrased in TOK vocabulary. TOK vocabulary refers to the terms and concepts that are specific to unpacking areas of knowledge and ways of knowing. TOK vocabulary includes all of the following words and more:

knower's perspective knowledge claim counter-claim concept language
evidence assumption knowledge belief truth faith logic
interpretation scope applications methodology judgement theory
explanation coherence wisdom argument fallacy certainty
probability justification implications perspectives historical context
historical development culture paradigm deductive reasoning
inductive reasoning areas of knowledge knowledge framework
shared and personal knowledge ways of knowing

> ★ It is important to phrase your knowledge question precisely. Once you have phrased your knowledge question well, you can then set about planning how you will present your analysis of it.

> ★ A knowledge question is always about knowledge, is open and is general. It should use TOK vocabulary, not the vocabulary related to the real-life situation.

Language

Real-life situation	Subject-specific question	Knowledge question
Uses any vocabulary and can be about any situation, school or community issues, national or international issues or subject-specific issue	Uses the vocabulary of a particular subject or area of knowledge and is a question that arises in a specific IB subject	Uses TOK vocabulary, is open-ended, comparative and is a question about knowing or knowledge

The International Space Station. What roles might reason, sense perception and imagination play in our pursuit of scientific knowledge?

Examples

Real-life situation	Subject-specific question	Knowledge question
The International Space Station is on the news.	How far is the scientific achievement of the ISS a product of international cooperation, scientific progress, reason and imagination?	How far does the pursuit of scientific knowledge depend on reason, sense perception and imagination?
An international university league table, Quacquarelli Symonds (QS), publishes a ranking of top universities.	How do the human sciences measure excellence?	To what extent are the measurements made in the human sciences and one other area of knowledge based on a reliable method?
A mathematician wins a Clay Mathematics Institute Prize for solving a long-standing mathematics problem.	What is the Poincaré conjecture and can we claim to know what the solution is?	To what extent is our knowledge the result of finding solutions to problems in mathematics, the arts and ethics?

Task: activity

1   Describe the features of and outline the differences between: (a) a real-life situation, (b) a subject-specific question and (c) a knowledge question.
2   Begin with a real-life situation, develop this into a subject-specific question and then develop it into a knowledge question.
3   Once you have developed your knowledge question, think of which areas of knowledge and which ways of knowing are relevant for you to explore in your presentation.

Make use of the TK/PPD Form that your teacher can find in the 'Handbook of procedures for the Diploma Programme'. This form should help you with your planning and needs to be filled in and given to your teacher before you give the presentation.

Summary

Extracting and formulating a knowledge question

- Clearly describe the real-life situation at the start of your presentation.
- Choose your own knowledge question that arises naturally from the real-life situation.
- Make sure your knowledge question is precisely worded and well formulated.

19 Developing a successful presentation

Introduction

This chapter focuses on your application of TOK thinking. We look at *analysis* of your knowledge question and how to investigate different *perspectives*, so that you can continue the development of an excellent presentation.

Applying TOK thinking

The features of good analysis are common to presentations and essays.

Just as with the essay, the emphasis in a presentation is on the quality of analysis. There are no marks for communicating information or giving a description. Use description concisely to support your insightful analysis. Analysis is key. 'Development' and 'progression' involves applying the following to your knowledge question: TOK *concepts, arguments, examples, perspectives* and related *knowledge questions*. The insights and conclusions reached are applied back to the original real-life situation and other situations. There are a number of ways to do this, as we can see in the following examples.

> 1 Three students began with a news story about a model who was rejected by a magazine for being 'too thin'. They used this real-life situation to think about the nature of beauty. Their knowledge question was about the *nature of truth in the arts and mathematics*. They looked at it from the perspectives of different cultural and historical conceptions of beauty. They explored the connections between beauty in mathematics and the arts and the different methods used to arrive at knowledge in each. Their examples included the use of the Fibonacci sequence and the golden ratio. Their approach was to look at the arguments for and against the idea that truth is discovered in mathematics and the arts. They performed a dialogue where one student put the arguments for truth being invented, the second put the case for truth being discovered and the third student presented a critical commentary on the strength and weaknesses of the arguments.

2   A pair of students chose a story in the news about the death penalty that focused on a particular case. Their knowledge question was to do with the roles of faith, reason and emotion in ethics and religious knowledge systems. One argued that the death penalty was justified and the other argued that it was not, and they concluded that the use of reason alone cannot be used as the basis for our knowledge in ethics. They looked at it from the perspectives of religious knowledge systems and ethics. They applied their insights and conclusions to other real-life situations involving life and death issues, including abortion and euthanasia. They also considered the implications of their argument that 'reason alone cannot be used as the basis for our knowledge' in other areas of knowledge. They organised their presentation so that they kept taking it in turns to speak, each for about two minutes at a time.

3   An individual student looked at a real-life situation based on the observation of the science writer Marcus Chown, that after 350 years of science we have come up with theories such as the Big Bang based on the 2% of the universe that we have seen. He heard this on a radio broadcast of a BBC science-themed comedy series, *The Infinite Monkey Cage*, in which it was outlined that we know that 98% of the universe is invisible to us. Most of the mass energy of the universe is made up of dark energy (73%) and dark matter (23%), which is invisible and gives out so little light we can't detect it. Only 4% of the universe is made of atoms but we have only seen half of that with telescopes. The student's knowledge question was to do with the scope and applications of science and the limitations of our knowledge in science and the arts. Science points to the limitation of our knowledge, and art might be able to communicate this insight into our shared 'known unknowns'. Through text, painting and film, the arts can communicate this sense very well. The student looked at it from the perspectives of different cultures and different points in history, making use of visual material and PowerPoint slides.

TOK concepts

You need to apply your own critical thinking to your knowledge question. Look at the TOK vocabulary list on page 154 and think of how different TOK ideas and concepts relate to your knowledge question. Select some TOK ideas and concepts to address in your presentation, for example identify **assumptions** and **fallacies** (errors in reasoning) and consider their implications.

Investigating multiple viewpoints and perspectives

You are required to identify, explore and evaluate different perspectives on your knowledge question. Think about how your knowledge question can be approached from different perspectives.

> ★ Make use of the knowledge framework to support your analysis of your knowledge question: scope and applications, key concepts, methods, historical development and links with personal knowledge.

> **assumption**: something that is supposed, presumed or taken for granted; an assumption can be hidden and 'implicit' or more obvious and 'explicit'
>
> **fallacies**: mistakes in reasoning

> ⓘ Examples of assumptions and fallacies include: hasty generalisations (making a 'big claim' that is not easily supported); *ad hominem* (supporting or attacking the person rather than their argument), *post hoc ergo propter hoc* (assuming there is a causal relationship between two things when there is only a correlation).

There are many ways that you might think about a real-life example such as a pair of swans. Different areas of knowledge will make various knowledge claims about swans. Biologists might claim knowledge of a swan's genus or natural history whereas a poet might represent swans as a symbol of love and fidelity. Just as you can look at a real-life example from many perspectives, you can also explore your knowledge question from different perspectives.

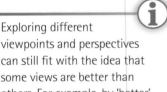

Exploring different viewpoints and perspectives can still fit with the idea that some views are better than others. For example, by 'better' we could mean that some viewpoints are based on a stronger justification than others, or by 'better' we might mean that some viewpoints have more useful applications than others. Rather than describing different perspectives on a knowledge question, take an analytical approach and weigh up the strengths and weaknesses of viewpoints. The key is to use your own judgement and discernment.

Task: think about

Consider different perspectives on the following. The heart might be thought of in biology as a pump for blood, but in literature a symbol of love. Both are 'correct' in their own subject-specific context. Think of subject-specific perspectives as well as different perspectives people may have as a result of their age, social class, cultural background, or the country they are raised in.

- A pair of swans
- A sunset
- The birth of a child
- A coin being flipped
- The human heart
- The discovery of the Higgs boson particle

Task: activity

In a presentation you might discuss one of the following knowledge claims:

1. Knowledge that is discovered by us is more certain than knowledge that is invented.
2. Within the context of economics and religious knowledge systems, faith and reason go together.
3. Imagination and creativity are needed to gain knowledge in both the arts and mathematics.
4. The concept of a hypothesis is equally important in science and history.
5. There are many factors that shape our knowledge gained through sense perception including language, expectation and how we feel.
6. In mathematics and science there is a clear distinction between proof and certain knowledge.
7. Our knowledge in science and history is based on spotting patterns.
   a. Think of several different cultural perspectives that you could explore.
   b. Think of several examples that you could use to support or oppose these points.

Example 1

Real-life situation: Group behaviour of the Japanese macaque monkey species

Subject-specific question: Can we predict how animals will behave in groups?

Knowledge question: Are we justified in thinking that we can use reason to predict behaviour in human science?

Analysis and insights:

Human behaviour is arguably unpredictable. Various psychological experiments successfully describe human tendencies that indicate reliable knowledge of how humans are likely to behave in some circumstances. In an experiment performed by American psychologist Solomon Asch in the 1950s, a group of people were given a set of test questions. Most of the group had been previously instructed to give incorrect answers, and the individual who was unknowingly the subject of the experiment felt obliged to give answers they knew were wrong in order to conform with the 'wisdom' of the crowd. This suggests that we are in a sense predictable; we are likely to disregard our own individual knowledge of what is correct in favour of the group consensus, even when we strongly suspect that the group is wrong. The implication here is that peer group pressure can be more influential than our own judgement in some group situations.

To reach a tentative conclusion, in human science, an experiment may count as evidence of a degree of predictability in terms of how humans are likely to behave in relation to their peer group.

Example 2

Real-life situation: Super-cooled helium, which in some cases seems to defy gravity

Subject-specific question: What methods are used in quantum mechanics to gain knowledge of subatomic particles?

Knowledge question: Can we be sure that the scientific method and the historical method are equally reliable?

Analysis and insights:

Science is sometimes claimed to be an area of knowledge which is not entirely reliable since our scientific knowledge is based on what has not yet been falsified. On the other hand, science could also be argued to be one of the most reliable routes to knowledge as the scientific method allows for mistaken knowledge to be rejected – this is called falsification.

Our preconceived ideas about science and the relative reliability of the inductive method may also determine our conclusions in other areas of knowledge. If we agree with a more sceptical conclusion about the unreliability of the scientific method it might follow that we might also be sceptical about historical knowledge. Our conclusions might to varying degrees be well-founded generalisations based on individual instances. Our individual perspective, culture and values will also shape what we think.

Applying your conclusion 'back' to your real-life situation

Your insights and conclusions can be applied back to your original real-life situation. Revisit your initial real-life situation and consider how you think about it differently now.

If your knowledge question was about whether it is justified to think that we can predict human behaviour and you have concluded that psychological experiments give us a reliable measure of how we are likely to act, you still need to relate it back to your initial real-life situation. If you conclude that humans are largely predictable, what does this mean for the Japanese macaques described in the TV documentary? What are the implications? Applying your insight back to the real-life situation it seems that like other animals we too have predictable behaviour. What makes us different is our use of reason, our ability to pass on knowledge. There will always be a limit to how well we can predict each other's behaviour. The nature of our freedom makes it impossible to calculate the future, which raises a new knowledge question about our knowledge of freedom.

Applying your conclusion 'forward' to other real-life situations

Your insights and conclusions can be applied forward to other real-life situations. What are the related situations? How might your conclusion affect the way you think about these other real-life situations?

A related situation to the macaques example might be predicting our spending habits: economists might forecast how we will spend our money. Another situation involves our personal intuition that we are in some ways unique but we feel the pressure to conform to conventions in many social situations. Related situations could include examples of peer group pressure, various types of conformity in the way we think and act, and the idea of the collective 'wisdom of crowds'. The presentation could end with a fresh critique of the philosopher Rousseau's observation that people were once born free, but in the course of history, society has limited our freedom, so that metaphorically we live 'in chains'. Just like the macaques, we have a tendency to obey rules beyond our reason and our own choosing.

You can also take your insights and conclusions and apply them forward to other parts of the TOK diagram. If your conclusion is that we cannot use reason to predict human behaviour you might also consider the impact of this conclusion on other areas of knowledge. In History, can we assume that the behaviour of individuals from the past is either rational or predictable? In economics can models forecast what we will buy? In ethics what difference does it make to our judgement of good and bad actions if we claim that our freedom is limited?

Summary

Applying TOK thinking

Use these questions to develop your thinking about your knowledge question. You might also make up and add your own questions to this list – developing the quality of your own critical thinking and questioning is one of the aims of TOK.

1 What is my real-life situation and knowledge question?
How are they connected? Does the knowledge question arise naturally from the real-life situation?

2 What are the different 'sides' to the knowledge question?
Make sure that there are at least two plausible alternatives.

3 What is the evidence?
Weigh up and evaluate the strength of evidence. How certain is it?

4 What are the links with areas of knowledge?
Choose two or more relevant areas of your choice.

5 What are the links with ways of knowing?
How do we know? Select some knowledge tools to make progress and explore possible answers.

6 What are the TOK principles and insights?
Bring out the TOK points you would like to make. Think of analytical points. Avoid descriptive points. What are your arguments? What are your own examples?

7 What is my tentative conclusion?
Include your own opinion and conclusion. You can agree with one side or neither. Don't be afraid to say what you think. Avoid conclusions that say nothing, such as 'There are different views on this question and it's just a matter of personal preference.'

8 What are other ways of looking at it?
Explore different cultural, social and intellectual approaches. What views might someone of a different age, social class or gender have? Take an open-minded approach. You don't have to agree with these other perspectives. There may be merit in different perspectives even if you don't share them.

9 What impact does my conclusion have on the way I think about my real-life situation?
Return to your real-life situation. Comment on what difference your insights, TOK principles and conclusions might have.

The following checklist sets out some of the ingredients that make up a good TOK presentation. Aim to include these features in your presentation.

Developing a successful presentation

- Analyse the knowledge question using examples and arguments.
- Develop excellent understanding of knowledge questions.
- Investigate ways to approach the topic from different perspectives.
- Explore and evaluate multiple viewpoints on the knowledge question.
- Use independent thought.
- Apply your insights and conclusions 'back' to your initial real-life situation.
- Think of other real-life situations that are similar or related.
- Apply your insights and conclusions 'forward' to these other real-life situations.

20 The basics: delivery and structuring your ideas

Introduction

In this chapter we set out to look at how you can put together your presentation and structure your ideas. We outline what makes a suitable introduction, development, use of examples and conclusion. There are also some tips on how to deliver your presentation.

Delivery

Think about the ways you want to get your points across effectively. You can use a number of techniques, and the presentation can take any format. Given that it is not permitted to deliver your presentation as a script or an essay that is read out, it's important to develop your own way of prompting yourself and remembering your next idea. Using flash cards is one way you can do this.

Remember that you are delivering the presentation and you cannot rely on the class to chip in or respond. It would be a weak and inappropriate approach to pose the knowledge question and then invite the class to say what they think and stand back. This would not count as an acceptable presentation. Your teacher may allow time for questions at the end but this is not a formal part of the presentation and you will not be assessed on your ability to field questions afterwards. So you need to make full and effective use of the time available to you.

You are not being assessed on your public speaking skills, but the following tips can make a crucial difference to the quality of your delivery. Depending on the size of the room, think about an appropriate level to project your voice. Keep facing the audience throughout the presentation and be sure to make eye contact with the group, which will maintain their interest. Present to your audience and if you are using visual material such as PowerPoint slides, avoid talking to the slides. Think about varying the tone of your voice and speaking at a suitable pitch. Be aware of your body language and hand gestures. Will you feel more comfortable sitting or standing? Will you need to move around? Think about the pace of your delivery; don't be afraid to pause. Have plenty of rehearsals until you feel confident.

> Consider preparing flash cards with a summary of bullet points. Use these cue cards as a prompt for the point you will talk about next.

Clarity

There are no marks for fluency, which is reassuring if you are giving the presentation in your second language. However, aim to communicate clearly so that your audience understands you. Speak clearly. Think about the pitch, pace and tone of your voice. Pause when you need to. Vary the tone of your voice to avoid speaking in a monotone.

Nerves

If you are likely to be nervous, think of techniques that will help you on the day:

- Breathe slowly and deeply – steady breathing helps your body to relax and calms your mind.
- Have some water with you to sip in case your throat gets dry.
- Visualise holding hands with someone you trust.
- Try to enjoy what you are doing; stay relaxed and calm.
- Build your confidence by taking opportunities for smaller mini-presentations during the course.

> ★
> You can give a very effective presentation on an interesting topic that nevertheless scores very poorly against the holistic TOK criteria. Remember that the presentation has to focus on an analysis of a knowledge question. The aim is to relate TOK thinking to the real world.

Structure

Present your ideas in a clear sequence. Use the four stages of planning set out by the IB diagram shown on page 147. You can't go far wrong if you use this for planning. Take your time to think about where to start with your audience. It's usual to begin with your real-life situation and knowledge question. For an individual presentation, aim to find around four to six analytical points to explore. Use each point in turn to develop your argument.

One technique is to *state* your point, *explain* it, give an *example*, consider it from another *perspective*, reach a *tentative conclusion* and then *apply it* back to the real-life situation. Alternative techniques are to shorten or vary this order.

The introduction

The presentation is an opportunity to demonstrate your critical thinking to the class. You will be speaking to your peer group in a classroom situation. It's important to get their attention from the start. A suitable introduction would be to outline your real-life situation and state the knowledge question you have extracted from it and explain the connection between the two.

There are a number of ways of doing this. If your real-life situation is based on a news story, you could show a clip of film from the news relating to it, or start with an image of the news story projected onto a screen and talk about the story, or read aloud an extract from a newspaper or website. You could use a visual aid or an artefact. You might use PowerPoint slides to describe your real-life situation and state your knowledge question.

When you mention your knowledge question it helps to pause; particularly if you have a long knowledge question, make sure that your audience has enough time to make a note of it mentally or on paper. Your class might be writing notes.

It will also help your audience if they know the scope and direction of your presentation in terms of any subsidiary knowledge questions, areas of knowledge, ways of knowing, arguments and perspectives. You could begin with a sketch or a dialogue that you perform.

Originality

There are many ways to present your topic in an original way. Including a *debate* in your presentation is one possible approach. If you are presenting in a pair, you can take your knowledge question and script a debate or dialogue, with one of you proposing one position or 'side' to the knowledge question (say the arguments for) and the other student in the pair putting the other position or 'side' (say the arguments against). Performing your debate would be a way of presenting the arguments in an engaging way. You could develop your analysis further by presenting a critical commentary on your debate; step back and revisit certain arguments, weighing up their relative merits. In your critical commentary you could identify any assumptions made in the different arguments and their implications. This approach could help you analyse and get 'under the skin' of the knowledge question and avoid a descriptive approach.

Another technique to present your ideas in a fresh and original way is to present an *interview* with pre-prepared questions and answers. Again you could comment critically afterwards on the questions and answers given. Alternatively you could include some drama, perform a sketch, act something out, use a mime, or get the audience involved by setting them a quiz or asking them to respond, for example to predict an outcome, or asking for a show of hands in response to a question. The presentation is open to creativity so you don't have to have a mechanical or predictable approach. Think about how to get your points across in a way that's thoughtful, engaging and inspired.

Guidance from your teacher

You are allowed to have one or two planning meetings with your teacher. Their role is to support you and help you plan your presentation. You need to agree on a time to deliver your presentation. Whilst they can advise you, the details must be your own decision, so that you choose the real-life situation, the knowledge question and the way you will approach them. The presentation is a key part of your intellectual journey and it should be the fruit of your independent learning supported and advised by your teacher. You are allowed to arrange an additional (third) meeting closer to your presentation time.

Planning and practice

You will need to plan what you are going to say and how you are going to say it. Just as with your essay, you need a clear structure. Begin planning on paper and get your ideas down.

If you are working in a pair or a group of three decide on the division of work; for variety you might take small sections each and speak for a few minutes at a time before swapping. If it is just you presenting think about the pace. If suitable and appropriate to your topic, should you show a film clip or play music to break the presentation up.

Take opportunities during the course to have a practice to help you decide what will suit you best in the final presentation. It's worth practising your presentation many times until you feel confident.

"Always start your presentation with a joke, but be careful not to offend anyone! Don't mention religion, politics, race, money, disease, technology, men, women, children, plants, animals, food..."

> Taking an original, personal and analytical approach is recommended.

Use of slides and visual material

You could use a prop or an artefact to illustrate a point. PowerPoint slides, possibly set to music, could make up part of your presentation. The slides are not the presentation; you are. However, with careful thinking, slides can be used effectively. Think about what will work to get your points across. Consider these two uses for your slides: (1) as your own prompts for what you will talk about next, or (2) as a summary of the key points you are making.

Think about your audience and make slides that will help keep your points clear and precise. Rather than make slides with lots of text, make effective use of images and pictures that can fill the whole slide. Make use of visual material when you put together your slides. If you are making a point about knowledge and art, a whole slide that shows one painting whilst you talk about it critically could be more effective than a slide with lots of writing. Where possible avoid slides with too much text. Certainly avoid reading whole chunks of text from projected slides as you are not allowed to do this.

Examples, quotations and film clips

Your own perspective and examples are much more valuable than any that you will find in this book. Avoid using examples from here and instead draw on your own experiences and your own IB subjects. Avoid using obvious or typical examples. In mathematics never use the simplistic example $1 + 1 = 2$; instead use examples based on what you know, for example about vectors, sets, groups, matrices and functions. In the arts use examples from the novels, poetry and prose you have read in your Group 1 course.

The *knower's perspective* involves drawing on your own personal experience and examples. Use original and personal examples that are based on your own experience. This will make your perspective and own voice clear. Avoid using quotations as a 'proof'. Avoid the temptation to say: 'Aristotle claimed that *x* was the case', suggesting that it must therefore be true. If you use a quotation give your own critical comment on it. Similarly you can make effective use of film clips, say from YouTube, but it is best to make your own critical comments in response to them. Use them to make a TOK point. Making analytical points is key.

> If you make use of a film clip use it effectively, for example to make an analytical point. Your thinking and analysis of the clip are important.

Handling opposing and different viewpoints

One important feature of a good presentation is that it will examine the knowledge question in the light of different perspectives. Think about your use of examples and arguments to support your analysis of the knowledge question. As with the essay, the same points apply: use examples to support analysis, and use fresh, personal examples from your own learning experience.

Just as with the essay it is very likely that your presentation will address and weigh up opposing and different viewpoints. You can write and perform a pre-prepared dialogue to present different viewpoints. This is an effective way to get a sense of the different positions you could adopt. You might also give a critical commentary during or after the dialogue to evaluate the strengths and weaknesses of the different positions.

An alternative approach is to make use of slides to get your points across. For example if there are three different positions you could adopt in response to your knowledge question, you might make a slide for each of the positions with clear text that outlines each position. You could then talk analytically about the slide, explain your point and give a sense of the relative merits of each position.

If you are handling different views, remember to arrive at a conclusion, even if it's a tentative one. Aim to get your points across clearly, making sure that you avoid the pitfall of presenting a mash of ideas without a clear conclusion. Avoid a lazy relativism that goes along the lines of: 'Here are the three different views which are all equally improbable; I'll leave it up to my audience to make up their own minds.'

Handling implications

Avoid the pitfall of stating your conclusion at the end and leaving it there. Towards the end of your presentation it is important to think through the implications that your argument has. The diagram on page 147 illustrates how you need to apply your conclusion elsewhere. This is what is meant by implications. Apply your conclusion 'back' to your real-life situation and 'forward' to other real-life situations.

Considering implications involves thinking through the logical conclusion of a knowledge claim or an argument. It involves asking: what next, or what follows? If in your presentation you come to the conclusion that our knowledge in science is not as certain as we might first assume, what follows? If scientific theories are those which have not yet been falsified, does it follow that our knowledge is strong or weak? What are the implications of this argument for the arts? If we challenge popular assumptions about science, what would happen if we challenge popular assumptions in other subject areas? Does it follow that our knowledge in the arts is more certain than we might first assume? These have to be your own judgements. Assumptions and implications are also dealt with in the context of the essay in Chapter 14.

Task: think about

In a presentation you might use quotations such as the following.
- 'Every man takes the limits of his own field of vision for the limits of the world.' (Schopenhauer)
- 'In expanding the field of knowledge we but increase the horizon of ignorance.' (Henry Miller)

Identify the *assumptions* behind, and the *implications* beyond, these two quotations and then do the same using other quotations.

The conclusion

Towards the end of the presentation, give a brief summary of the main points and then return to your real-life situation and apply your insights and conclusions back to it. You will also identify related real-life situations and again apply your insights and conclusion to those situations.

In your conclusion you need to step back from your own perspective and grasp the *implications* of what you are saying. End with a forward-looking view. How might you think differently now as a result of your critical thinking? Are there unresolved questions or new knowledge questions that have arisen?

- Try to watch an exemplar presentation. They are available to your teacher on the OCC website. Your school might also keep recordings of presentations given by previous candidates at your school. You could try marking them yourself against the holistic marking criteria.
- As with your essay you need to acknowledge the ideas of other people; you are not allowed to pass off other people's ideas as your own.

Task: activity

1 Watch an exemplar presentation that your teacher can gain access to from the IB Online Curriculum Centre (OCC) and award it marks against the holistic criteria.
2 Compare your comments with those made by examiners.

Summary

What the presentation is	What the presentation is not
a *summative* assessment of your learning and a *formative* part of the TOK course for your class	a test
part of your own intellectual journey	a presentation of research or information
approached from your own knower's perspective and experience	exclusively about key thinkers or philosophers
a dialogue that makes connections between the real world and the world of TOK thinking	a description or report on an interesting topic
your delivery of a presentation with planned content that you deliver individually or in a pair or group of three	a question posed to the class for them to discuss and have an open dialogue with you
a presentation spoken 'live' to the group	read from an essay or pre-recorded and the film shown to the class

Index